# Pillsbury Kids Cookbook

Food
Fun for
Boys
and
Girls

WILEY

Wiley Publishing, Inc.

Copyright © 2005 by General Mills, Minneapolis, MN
All rights reserved.

Published by Wiley Publishing, Inc., Hoboken, NJ

No part of this publication may be reproduced, stored in a retrieval
system, or transmitted in any form or by any means, electronic,
mechanical, photocopying, recording, scanning or otherwise, except as
permitted under Sections 107 or 108 of the 1976 United States
Copyright Act, without either the prior written permission of the
Publisher or authorization through payment of the appropriate per-
copy fee to the Copyright Clearance Center, 222 Rosewood Drive,
Danvers, MA 01923, (978) 750-8400, fax (978) 646-8600. Requests
to the Publisher for permission should be addressed to the
Permissions Department, John Wiley & Sons, Inc. 111 River Street,
Hoboken, NY 07030, (201) 748-0611, fax 201-748-6008, or online at
http://www.wiley.com/go/permission.

Trademarks: Wiley and the Wiley Publishing logo are trademarks or
registered trademarks of John Wiley & Sons and/or its affiliates. All
other trademarks referred to herein are trademarks of General Mills,
or its subsidiaries. Wiley Publishing, Inc., is not associated with any
product or vendor mentioned in this book.

Limit of Liability/Disclaimer of Warranty: While the publisher and
author have used their best efforts in preparing this book, they make no
representations or warranties with respect to the accuracy or
completeness of the contents of this book and specifically disclaim any
implied warranties of merchantability or fitness for a particular
purpose. No warranty may be created or extended by sales
representatives or written sales materials. The advice and strategies
contained herein may not be suitable for your situation. You should
consult with a professional where appropriate. Neither the publisher
nor author shall be liable for any loss of profit or any other commercial
damages, including but not limited to special, incidental,
consequential, or other damages.

For general information on our other products and services or to
obtain technical support, please, contact our Customer Care
Department within the U.S. at 800-762-2974 and outside the U.S. at
317-572-3993 or fax 317-572-4002.

Wiley also publishes its books in a variety of electronic formats. Some
content that appears in print may not be available in electronic books.

**Library of Congress Cataloging-in-Publication Data:**

Pillsbury kids cookbook : food fun for boys and girls.
    p. cm.
Includes index.
ISBN-13: 978-0-470-07911-9 (pbk.)
ISBN-10: 0-470-07911-8 (pbk.)
1.  Cookery—Juvenile literature.  I. Title: Cookbook for kids. II.
Pillsbury Company.
 TX652.5.P5 2005
 641.5'123—dc22

                        2005000846

Manufactured in China

10 9 8 7 6 5 4 3 2 1

**General Mills**
Director, Book and Online Publishing: Kim Walter
Manager, Cookbook Publishing: Lois Tlusty
Editor: Heidi Losleben
Recipe Development and Testing: Pillsbury Kitchens
Photography and Food Styling: General Mills Photography Studios

**Wiley Publishing, Inc.**
Publisher: Natalie Chapman
Executive Editor: Anne Ficklen
Editor: Kristi Hart
Production Editor: Ava Wilder
Cover Design: Suzanne Sunwoo
Interior Design and Layout: Platinum Design Inc., NYC
Photography Art Direction: Pam Kurtz
Manufacturing Manager: Kevin Watt

Cover photo: Fruity Banana Smoothies (page 20)

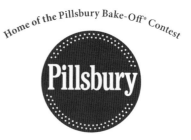

*Our recipes have been
tested in the Pillsbury Kitchens
and meet our standards of easy
preparation, reliability and great taste.*

For more great recipes, visit pillsbury.com

# For Kids Only!

Congratulations! You are the proud owner of your very own cookbook. What are you going to make first? The Silly Snake Dogs (page 48) look pretty fun; so do the Alphabet Dunkers (page 122). Then again, why not skip straight to dessert and make some yummy Glazed Brownie Hearts (page 154)?

Whatever recipe you decide to start with, it's a good idea to read the beginning part of this book first. The safety tips will keep you from getting hurt, and the helpful hints will make your time in the kitchen go smoothly.

If you are confused by a direction in a recipe or don't know what kind of tool to use or how to use it, check out the inside pages of the front and back covers and pages 8 and 9. And remember, if a recipe calls for a sharp tool or something hot, always ask an adult for help. It's not cheating—even famous chefs on TV and in restaurants have helpers in the kitchen. You can still say "I did it!" after the food is made (in fact, that's the very best part).

Good luck and happy cooking!

The Pillsbury Editors

# Contents

# Kitchen ABCs

## Let's Get Cooking

Are you ready to mix up some muffins? Stir up a smoothie? Put together a pizza boat? Well, there are a few things to think about before you're up to your eyeballs in good eats!

### On Your Mark . . .

* It's a good idea to put on an apron or an old shirt (with the sleeves rolled up) before you start cooking. That way, your clothes stay clean. If you have long hair, you may want to tie it back, away from your face.

* Wash your hands with soap and water, and dry them with a clean towel to keep germs away from the food.

### Get Set . . .

* Read over the whole recipe with your adult helper before you start. Make sure you understand the directions and that you have all the ingredients you need to make the recipe.

* Set out all the ingredients and utensils you'll need on a tray. That way, everything will be ready when you need it and you won't waste time hunting around.

### . . . Go!

* Remember to watch for the ✦ symbol. Even if you think you can do what the recipe says, it's important to have an adult close by, just in case.

* Clean up as you go. Then you won't have such a big mess at the end and you can get to the tasting part faster!

# Healthy, Wealthy and Wise

It's important to take good care of your body because it's the only one you've got! Knowing what nutrients are in the food you eat can help you stay ship-shape. Here's how to decode the nutrition info at the bottom of each recipe page. The amount you need of each of these things depends on how old you are and how much exercise you get. Doctors and other grown-ups know lots about this stuff. Talk to them if you have questions.

✳ **Calories** come from the protein, carbohydrates and fat in food. Calories provide energy for your body, but if you eat more calories than your body uses, you gain weight.

✳ **Fat** sounds like it's a bad thing, but your body actually needs some fat to work correctly. Fat cushions your organs, keeps your body warm and helps you have healthy skin and hair.

✳ **Sodium** is pretty much the same thing as salt. Some people have to be super-careful not to get a lot of sodium in their food, otherwise they'll get high blood pressure.

✳ **Carbohydrates** are sometimes called "carbs." Carbs are needed because they provide fuel (or energy) to the cells in your body. Some carbs give your body energy fast, while other kinds give you energy more slowly.

✳ **Sugar** is a simple carb (see above). Even though sugar tastes good, you don't want too much of it or you'll get cavities.

✳ **Protein** helps your muscles, blood and organs to build, maintain and repair themselves. If you take your weight and divide it by 2, that's about how many grams of protein you need a day.

# Cooking Terms and Techniques

Are you ready to cook? Well, first it's important to learn the lingo. What's the difference between grating and shredding? How about chopping and slicing? Do you know how to crack open an egg? Read on to find out.

**Bake:** Cook food in an oven.

**Beat:** Make a mixture smooth by quickly stirring the ingredients in a circle.

**Boil:** Heat liquid in a saucepan on top of the stove until big bubbles come up to the top and burst open.

**Brown:** Cook food on top of the stove, under a broiler or in an oven until it looks brown on the outside.

**Chill:** Put food in the refrigerator until it gets cold.

**Chop:** Cut food into little pieces with a sharp knife on a cutting board. The pieces should be about the same size, but it's okay if they're not all exactly the same shape. (See the How-To Photo below.)

Chop  Slice

Shred

**Cool:** Put food on a wire rack or set it on a hot pad on the counter until it is no longer warm when you touch it.

**Cover:** Put a lid or piece of foil or plastic wrap over food.

**Crack Open an Egg:** Hold an egg in one hand and tap it firmly on the rim of a custard cup or small bowl. Make the crack a little bigger with your thumbs and slowly pull the two halves of the eggshell apart. (See the How-To Photo, page 154.) Let the white and yolk drop into the custard cup or bowl. Make sure to pick out any pieces of eggshell that fall into the cup or bowl before you add other ingredients.

**Drain:** Pour food with liquid in a strainer or colander so the liquid runs through the holes of the strainer or colander.

**Fold:** Put a rubber spatula straight down into a mixture and gently scrape it along the bottom of the bowl and up the side toward you, kind of like you are trying to turn the mixture upside down. Every time you do this, turn the bowl a little with your other hand. You want to keep the mixture as light and fluffy as possible.

**Freeze:** Put food in the freezer until it is very hard.

**Grate:** Rub an ingredient against the side of the grater that has the rough little poke-outs on it. You wind up with very tiny pieces.

**Grease:** Spread vegetable shortening on the bottom, and sometimes sides, of a pan to keep food from sticking. (Vegetable shortening comes in a can and is thick and white.) You can also use cooking spray.

**Measure Dry Ingredients:** Use a dry measuring cup to measure out ingredients like flour, sugar and cereal. (See the How-To Photo, page 42.) Dry measuring cups come in different sizes and fit into each other. Spoon the ingredient into the measuring cup. Use the straight edge of a table knife to make the top level.

**Measure Liquid Ingredients:** Use a liquid (see-through) measuring cup with a spout to measure liquids like water or milk. Set the liquid measuring cup on a flat surface. Pour in the liquid. Then bend down or stand on your tiptoes so you can read the amount on the cup.

**Measure Small Amounts of Ingredients:** Use a measuring spoon to measure small amounts of ingredients like vanilla, baking powder and spices. (See the How-To Photo, page 82.) Dip the measuring spoon into dry ingredients, and level off the top with the straight edge of a table knife. Pour liquid ingredients into the spoon.

**Melt:** Heat a solid ingredient, such as butter, over low heat until it turns into a liquid.

**Mix or Stir:** Combine ingredients together until they are smooth or almost smooth.

**Peel:** Remove the outer layer, or skin, of a fruit or vegetable.

**Roll:** Flatten out a ball of dough with a rolling pin.

**Separate an Egg:** Rest an egg separator over the top of a custard cup or small bowl. Hold an egg in one hand and tap it firmly on the rim of a custard cup or bowl. Make the crack a little bigger with your thumb and slowly pull the two halves of the eggshell apart. Let the yolk fall into the center of the egg separator. The white part of the egg will fall through the slots of the separator into the cup or bowl. (See the How-To Photo, page 144.)

**Shred:** Rub an ingredient against the side of the grater that has small or large holes with sharp edges on each hole. You wind up with skinny shreds of food. (See the How-To Photo, page 8.)

**Slice:** Cut food into flat pieces with a sharp knife on a cutting board. The pieces should be about the same thickness. (See the How-To Photo, page 8.)

# Play It Safe

The kitchen is a very fun place, but there are certain things you have to watch out for—like hot burners and sharp knives. These things aren't dangerous if you know how to use them. When you see this symbol 🧤, let your adult helper take over or watch you closely. Here are a few safety tips to keep in mind when you are cooking and baking.

### Hot, Hot, Hot!

* Burners can get very hot and so can the inside of the oven. Remember to be extra careful around these things and to use thick, dry pot holders or hot pads whenever you touch a pan, pot or food that has just come off a hot burner, out of the oven or out of the microwave.

* Remember to roll up your sleeves and to watch your hands, arms and wrists around hot burners and stoves.

* If you are stirring something on top of the stove, use a wooden spoon, not a metal one. A metal spoon will get hot like the pan, but a wooden spoon will stay cool.

* Boiling water is very, very hot, so be sure to ask an adult helper to lend you a hand if a recipe tells you to boil water.

* Steam coming off the top of boiling water is also very hot. If you need to remove the lid from a pan of boiling water, tip the lid away from you.

* Point the handles of pots and pans toward the center of the stove so you don't bump them and spill hot food. Make sure the handles aren't over another burner.

* If you have to stand on your tip toes to reach the microwave, it's a good idea to ask an adult helper to do the microwave stuff.

## Cut It Out

✳ Before you cut, chop or slice any foods, ask your adult helper if it is okay. A lot of times, cooking or baking goes much faster if you let your adult helper deal with the sharp stuff.

✳ If your adult helper says it's okay to use a sharp knife, remember to turn the blade away from you and to keep your fingers out of the way.

✳ Always use a cutting board when you cut, chop or slice foods. Your adult helper wants you to leave your mark in the world—just not on the countertop.

## Don't Get Zapped!

✳ Before you try to scrape the sides of the blender container, turn the blender off and unplug it by pulling on the plug, not the cord. Remember to put the lid on before you turn the blender back on, or you will have a mess!

✳ Turn off and unplug the electric mixer before you scrape the side of the bowl or take the beaters out.

✳ Electricity and water don't mix, so keep all electrical appliances away from water, and make sure your hands are dry when you use them.

✳ Make sure to use microwave-safe dishes and pans in the microwave. Metal and microwaves is a bad combo. Combine them and . . . look out! Sparks will fly (not in a good way).

# Rise &

# Shine

## Eight yummy reasons to bounce out of bed

# Strawberry-Kiwi Parfait

TIME IT TAKES: 10 minutes • HOW MUCH IT MAKES: 1 parfait

## INGREDIENTS

1/2 cup Honey
  NutClusters® cereal
1 small kiwifruit
1 container (6 ounces)
  strawberry-mango
  low-fat yogurt

## TOOLS YOU NEED

• Measuring cups
• Sharp knife
• Cutting board
• Spoon
• Clear drinking glass
  (10 ounce)

**1** Measure out the cereal.

**2** Use the knife to cut off the fuzzy brown part of the kiwifruit on the cutting board. Cut the kiwifruit into small pieces.

**3** Spoon about half of the yogurt into the drinking glass.

**4** Use the knife to cut off the fuzzy brown part of the kiwifruit on the cutting board. Cut the kiwifruit into small pieces.

**5** Spoon about half of the yogurt into the drinking glass.

**6** Top the yogurt with half of the kiwifruit and half of the cereal. Do this again with the other half of the yogurt, kiwifruit and cereal.

*1 Parfait:* Calories 330; Total Fat 3 1/2 g; Sodium 230mg; Total Carbohydrates 67g (Sugars 44g); Protein 10g • *Exchanges:* 1 Fruit, 2 Other Carbohydrates, 1 Low-Fat Milk

**PERSONALIZE YOUR PARFAIT**
Create your own version of this fruity parfait by using whatever kind of yogurt is your favorite. Or, try using blueberries or cut-up mango pieces instead of kiwifruit.

# Cheesy Apple Chunk Bagels

**TIME IT TAKES:** 20 minutes • **HOW MUCH IT MAKES:** 4 bagel halves

## INGREDIENTS

1/4 cup strawberry
cream cheese spread

1 medium apple

1 banana

2 bagels (pick your
favorite flavor)

## TOOLS YOU NEED

- Measuring cups
- Small bowl
- Rubber spatula
- Spoon
- Sharp knife
- Cutting board
- Table knife
- Serrated knife
- Toaster or toaster
oven

**1** Measure out the cream cheese spread. Put it in the bowl. Scrape all of it out of the measuring cup with the rubber spatula. Stir the cream cheese spread with the spoon until it is soft and creamy.

**2** Use the sharp knife to cut the apple in half from top to bottom on the cutting board. Cut each half in half again. Cut out the seeds in the middle of 1 quarter. Cut the quarter into tiny pieces. (See the How-To Photo. You should get about 1/4 cup.) Eat the rest of the apple quarters later.

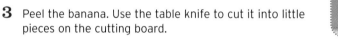

**3** Peel the banana. Use the table knife to cut it into little pieces on the cutting board.

**4** Add the apple and banana to the cream cheese spread in the bowl. Stir gently with the spoon to mix everything up.

**5** Use the serrated knife to cut each of the bagels in half to form 2 round halves on the cutting board. Toast each bagel half in the toaster or toaster oven.

**6** Spoon the cream cheese onto the toasted bagel halves. Spread it around with the table knife.

*1 Bagel Half:* Calories 160; Total Fat 6g; Sodium 200mg; Total Carbohydrates 24g (Sugars 6g); Protein 4g • *Exchanges:* 1 Starch, 1 Fat

> **GREAT GADGET**
> Before you use a knife to cut the bagels in half, see if you have a bagel splitter in the kitchen. If you do, ask a grown-up to show you how to use it.

# Sunny-Side Up Waffles

TIME IT TAKES: 15 minutes • HOW MUCH IT MAKES: 4 waffles

## INGREDIENTS

4 frozen homestyle or buttermilk waffles

2 containers (6 ounces each) vanilla thick and creamy low-fat yogurt

4 canned apricot halves

## TOOLS YOU NEED

• Toaster or toaster oven
• Pot holders
• 4 plates
• Spoon
• Can opener
• Paper towel

**1** Toast the frozen waffles in the toaster or toaster oven until they are warm. You might have to toast them more than one time.

**2** Carefully remove the waffles from the toaster with the pot holders. Put 1 waffle on each of the plates.

**3** Spoon about half of 1 container of yogurt onto each warm waffle. Smooth the yogurt around with the back of the spoon until it almost covers the top of each waffle.

**4** Open the can of apricots with the can opener. Take out 4 apricot halves. Put the apricots on a paper towel to drain off the juice. Put the rest of the apricots in the refrigerator to use some other time.

**5** Top each waffle with an apricot half, rounded side up.

*1 Waffle: Calories 220; Total Fat 4g; Sodium 340mg; Total Carbohydrates 40g (Sugars 21g); Protein 6g • Exchanges: 2 Starch*

### GO GOURMET
These look like fried eggs, don't they? Rather than using plain waffles, mix things up by substituting frozen blueberry or apple-cinnamon waffles instead. You could also use peach halves instead of apricot halves.

# Fruity Banana Smoothies

**TIME IT TAKES:** 15 minutes • **HOW MUCH IT MAKES:** 3 smoothies (1 cup each)

## INGREDIENTS

2 containers (8 ounces each) vanilla low-fat yogurt

1/4 cup orange juice

1 cup frozen whole strawberries

1 banana

1 1/2 teaspoons miniature semisweet chocolate chips or crushed Trix® cereal

## TOOLS YOU NEED

• Blender with lid
• Rubber spatula
• Liquid measuring cup (1 cup)
• Measuring cups
• Table knife
• Cutting board
• 3 drinking glasses (10 ounce)
• Measuring spoons

**1** Put the yogurt in the blender. Scrape all of it out of the containers with the rubber spatula.

**2** Measure out the orange juice in the liquid measuring cup. Pour it into the blender.

**3** Take the bag of frozen strawberries out of the freezer. Measure out 1 cup. Put the rest of the strawberries back in the freezer.

**4** Peel the banana. Use the table knife to cut it into chunks on the cutting board. Toss the banana chunks and the strawberries into the blender.

**5** Cover the blender with the lid. Blend until the mixture is smooth.

**6** Pour the mixture into the glasses so each has about the same amount. Measure out 1/2 taspoon of the chocolate chips. Sprinkle them on 1 of the smoothies. Repeat measuring the chips and putting them on the other 2 smoothies.

*1 Smoothie: Calories 230; Total Fat 2 1/2g; Sodium 90mg; Total Carbohydrates 47g (Sugars 38g); Protein 8g • **Exchanges:** 2 Starch, 1 Fruit*

**TASTY TOPPING**
Instead of topping these smoothies with chocolate chips or cereal, try cutting up your favorite fruit and sprinkling it on top of these great-tasting drinks, like on the cover of this book.

# S'more Hot Cereal

TIME IT TAKES: 10 minutes • HOW MUCH IT MAKES: 1 bowl of cereal

## INGREDIENTS

1/2 cup milk

1/4 cup water

3 tablespoons dry chocolate or regular flavor hot wheat cereal

2 tablespoons miniature marshmallows

2 tablespoons semisweet chocolate chips

1/4 cup Golden Grahams® cereal

**1** Measure out the milk in the liquid measuring cup. Pour it into the bowl. Measure out the water in the liquid measuring cup. Pour it into the bowl. Measure out the dry cereal. Pour it into the bowl, too.

**2** Follow the directions on the wheat cereal package to make the cereal in the microwave.

**3** While the cereal is getting hot, measure out the marshmallows and put them in the custard cup. Measure out the chocolate chips and put them in the same custard cup. Measure out the Golden Grahams.

**4** As soon as the cereal is done, use the spoon to stir in the marshmallows and the chocolate chips. Sprinkle the Golden Grahams on top.

*1 Bowl of Cereal:* Calories 340; Total Fat 10g; Sodium 160mg; Total Carbohydrates 56g (Sugars 24g); Protein 9g • *Exchanges:* 3 Starch, 1 Other Carbohydrate, 1 Fat

## TOOLS YOU NEED

• Liquid measuring cup (1 cup)
• Small microwavable bowl
• Measuring spoons
• Measuring cups
• Custard cup
• Spoon

**CHIP CHANGE**
You don't have to use chocolate chips if you don't want. If you really want to mix things up, try using cherry, raspberry or cinnamon chips instead.

# Banana-Oatmeal Surprise Mini Muffins

**TIME IT TAKES: 35 minutes  •  HOW MUCH IT MAKES: 24 mini muffins**

## INGREDIENTS

1 pouch (6.4 ounces) banana nut premium muffin mix

1/2 cup water

1/4 cup quick-cooking or old-fashioned oats

2 tablespoons vegetable oil

1 egg

24 milk chocolate chunks

## TOOLS YOU NEED

- 24 miniature paper baking cups
- 2 miniature muffin pans (with 12 cups in each)
- Cooking spray
- Medium bowl
- Liquid measuring cup (1 cup)
- Measuring cups
- Measuring spoons
- Wooden spoon
- Spoon
- Pot holders
- Wire cooling racks

1  Heat the oven to 350ºF.

2  Count out 24 miniature paper baking cups. Put them in the 24 cups in the muffin pans. Lightly spray the paper cups with cooking spray.

3  Pour the muffin mix from the pouch into the bowl. Measure out the water in the liquid measuring cup. Measure out the oats. Add the water and oats to the bowl. Measure out the oil. Add it to the bowl, too.

4  Carefully crack the egg on the edge of the bowl. Open the shell and let the egg slide into the bowl. Mix everything up with the wooden spoon.

5  Use the regular spoon to carefully fill each of the paper cup-lined muffin cups about 3/4 full with batter. Lightly press 1 chocolate chunk down into the batter in each cup until it disappears.

6  Bake the muffins for 16 to 18 minutes or until they look light golden brown and the tops puff back up when you touch them lightly in the center. Be careful when you touch the muffins so that you don't touch the hot oven.

7  Carefully take the muffin pans out of the oven with the pot holders. Put them on the wire racks. Let the muffins cool for 1 minute. Remove them from the pans. Cool the muffins about 5 minutes before eating them.

*1 Mini Muffin: Calories 70; Total Fat 3g; Sodium 45mg; Total Carbohydrates 9g (Sugars 4g); Protein 1g • Exchanges: Free*

**FREEZE IT!**
Unless you're feeding an army, you're probably going to have some muffins left over. Just put any extras in a freezer plastic bag and pop them in the freezer. Then, when you get the muffin munchies, nuke them in the microwave for about 10 seconds on High.

# Bunny Rabbit Pancakes

TIME IT TAKES: 10 minutes • HOW MUCH IT MAKES: 3 pancakes

## INGREDIENTS

1/4 cup maple-flavored pancake syrup

3 frozen original pancakes

8 raisins

1 maraschino cherry

2 pieces red string licorice (each 1 1/2 inches long)

## TOOLS YOU NEED

- Liquid measuring cup (1 cup)
- Microwavable plate
- Table knife
- Cutting board
- Pot holders

**1** Measure out the pancake syrup in the liquid measuring cup.

**2** Stack the pancakes on the plate. Microwave on High 30 seconds.

**3** Use the table knife to cut one of the pancakes into pieces for the ears and the bow tie on the cutting board. (See the How-To Photo for what the shapes should look like. The two outside pieces are the ears.) Arrange the ears and the bow tie around the stack of pancakes so it looks like a bunny.

**4** Microwave the pancakes on High 30 to 45 seconds, until the pancakes are warm all the way through. Carefully take the plate out of the microwave with the pot holders.

**5** To make the bunny's face, put 2 raisins on the top pancake where the eyes should be. Put the cherry where the nose should be. Use the string licorice to make the mouth. Put 3 raisins on each side of the bunny's bow tie. Drizzle syrup over the top.

*3 Pancakes:* Calories 470; Total Fat 3g; Sodium 810mg; Total Carbohydrates 105g (Sugars 36g); Protein 6g • **Exchanges:** 2 Starch, 5 Other Carbohydrates

> **GET CREATIVE**
> Instead of a bunny, try making other animals out of the pancakes. How about a dog or a cat? Can you think of other foods you could use to make the eyes, nose and mouth?

# Breakfast Biscuits

TIME IT TAKES: 45 minutes  •  HOW MUCH IT MAKES: 8 sandwiches

## INGREDIENTS

1 can (16.3 ounces)
 large refrigerated
 buttermilk biscuits

8 thin slices Canadian-
 style bacon (about
 4 1/2 ounces)

8 slices (1 ounce each)
 American cheese

## TOOLS YOU NEED

- Cookie sheet
- Pot holders
- Hot pad
- Serrated knife
- Cutting board
- Microwavable plastic
 wrap
- Resealable freezer
 plastic bags (1 gallon)

**1** Put the biscuits on the cookie sheet and bake them like the directions say on the can. When they're done baking, carefully take the cookie sheet out of the oven with the pot holders and set it on the hot pad on the kitchen counter. Let the biscuits cool 20 minutes or until they aren't warm anymore.

**2** Use the serrated knife to cut the biscuits in half sideways on the cutting board. Put 1 slice of Canadian bacon and 1 slice of cheese between each of the biscuit halves.

**3** Wrap each of the sandwiches up in the plastic wrap. Put all the sandwiches in the plastic bags and put the plastic bags in the freezer.

**4** When you are ready to eat a sandwich, take the plastic bag out of the freezer. Then take one sandwich out of the plastic bag and loosen the plastic wrap. Put the plastic bag with the rest of the sandwiches back in the freezer. Microwave the sandwich on High for 45 to 60 seconds or until it is hot all the way through and the cheese is melted. Let the sandwich cool 30 to 60 seconds before you eat it.

*1 Sandwich: Calories 330; Total Fat 18g; Sodium 1,300mg; Total Carbohydrates 28g (Sugars 9g); Protein 13g • Exchanges: 2 Starch, 1 High-Fat Meat, 2 Fat*

### TOPS IN TASTE
Don't forget about these breakfast biscuits once you put them in the freezer. Try to eat them within 3 months—otherwise they won't taste half as yummy.

# High

# Noon

## A bunch of great lunch ideas

# Grilled Cheese and Salsa

TIME IT TAKES: 30 minutes • HOW MUCH IT MAKES: 2 servings
(1 sandwich and 1/4 cup salsa each)

## INGREDIENTS

4 teaspoons softened
butter or margarine

4 slices whole wheat
or white bread

2 slices (3/4 ounce
each) American
cheese

2 slices (3/4 ounce
each) Muenster
cheese

1/2 cup chunky-style
salsa

## TOOLS YOU NEED

- Measuring spoons
- Table knife
- Large skillet
  (10 or 12 inch)
- Pancake turner
- Cutting board
- Measuring cups
- Spoon
- 2 custard cups
- Rubber spatula

1  Measure out 1 teaspoon of the softened butter. Use the table knife to spread it on 1 slice of bread. Repeat measuring the butter and spreading it on the other 3 slices of bread.

2  Put 2 slices of bread, butter side down, in the skillet. Put 1 slice of American cheese and 1 slice of Muenster cheese on top of each of these bread slices. Put the other 2 slices of bread, butter side up, on top of the cheese.

3  Cook the sandwiches in the skillet over medium heat for 2 to 4 minutes or until the bread on the bottom looks golden brown. (Use the pancake turner to peek underneath.) Flip the sandwiches over with the pancake turner. Cook another 2 to 4 minutes or until the other side looks golden brown. Use the pancake turner to remove the sandwiches from the skillet and put them on the cutting board. Let them cool for 5 minutes.

4  While the sandwiches are cooling, measure out the salsa. Spoon half of it into each custard cup. Scrape all the salsa out of the measuring cup with the rubber spatula.

5  Use the table knife to cut the sandwiches into strips or triangles. To eat, dip the sandwich pieces into the salsa.

*1 Serving: Calories 380; Total Fat 23g; Sodium 1,070mg; Total Carbohydrates 31g
(Sugars 5g); Protein 16g • Exchanges: 2 Starch, 2 Fat*

### GET CHEESY!
You can use whatever flavor of cheese you like most. Try experimenting with slices of mozzarella, Cheddar or even Swiss.

# Ham 'n Cheese Bites

**TIME IT TAKES:** 25 minutes • **HOW MUCH IT MAKES:** 4 servings (4 bites each)

## INGREDIENTS

1 package (2.5 ounces) thinly sliced cooked ham

4 slices white or whole wheat bread

4 sticks (1 ounce each) string cheese

1/2 cup honey mustard salad dressing

## TOOLS YOU NEED

• Table knife
• Cutting board
• Rolling pin
• 16 toothpicks
• Serrated knife
• Measuring cups
• Spoon
• 2 custard cups
• Rubber spatula

1 Divide the ham into 4 equal stacks. Use the table knife to cut the crusts off the bread on the cutting board.

2 Roll out each slice of bread with the rolling pin until it is about 1/4 inch thick. Put 1 stack of ham on each of the flattened slices of bread. Then put 1 stick of cheese on top of each stack of ham.

3 Roll up the slices of bread. Stick 4 toothpicks in each roll, spacing them about 1 inch apart. Put the rolls on the cutting board. Use the serrated knife to cut each roll into 4 pieces between the toothpicks.

4 Measure out the salad dressing. Spoon half of it into each custard cup. Scrape all the dressing out of the measuring cup with the rubber spatula. To eat, dip the sandwich bites into the salad dressing.

*4 Bites:* Calories 280; Total Fat 17g; Sodium 740mg; Total Carbohydrates 16g (Sugars 4g); Protein 14g • *Exchanges:* 1 Starch

### GRAB AND GO
You could make these roll-ups the night before and take them to school for lunch. Just wrap them in plastic wrap and store them in the refrigerator. Store the salad dressing in a plastic container with a lid. Remember to add an ice pack in your lunch bag to keep everything cool.

# Super Subs

TIME IT TAKES: 20 minutes  •  HOW MUCH IT MAKES: 4 sandwiches

## INGREDIENTS

4 hot dog or bratwurst
  buns
1/4 cup creamy Italian
  dressing
4 slices bologna
4 slices (3/4 ounce
  each) American
  cheese
2 plum (Roma)
  tomatoes
1/2 cup shredded
  lettuce

## TOOLS YOU NEED

• Serrated knife
• Cutting board
• Liquid measuring
  cup (1 cup)
• Table knife
• Sharp knife
• Measuring cups

1   If the hot dog buns aren't already split down the middle, use the serrated knife to cut them in half on the cutting board.

2   Measure out the dressing. Drizzle it equally over the cut sides of each of the buns. Use the table knife to cut each slice of bologna in half. Use the table knife again to cut each slice of cheese in half from one corner to the opposite corner to make 2 triangles.

3   Wash the tomatoes. Put 1 tomato on its side on the cutting board. Use the sharp knife to cut it into thin slices. Do the same with the other tomato. Measure out the lettuce.

4   For each sub sandwich, put 2 bologna halves on the bottom half of the bun. Then put 2 triangles of cheese on top of the bologna. Add a couple of slices of tomato. Sprinkle some lettuce on top of the tomato. Cover with the top half of the bun.

*1 Sandwich: Calories 360; Total Fat 23g; Sodium 980mg; Total Carbohydrates 26g (Sugars 4g); Protein 12g • **Exchanges:** 1 1/2 Starch, 1 High-Fat Meat, 3 Fat*

### TEAM EFFORT
These sandwiches are fun to make with 3 of your friends. One of you can be in charge of preparing the hot dog buns; someone can cut the bologna and cheese into pieces; another friend can slice the tomatoes; and someone else can measure out the lettuce.

# Sandwiches on a Stick

TIME IT TAKES: 40 minutes • HOW MUCH IT MAKES: 4 sandwiches

## INGREDIENTS

1/4 cup mayonnaise

2 tablespoons
  Thousand Island
  salad dressing

6 slices bacon

1 medium tomato

9 slices white or whole
  wheat sandwich
  bread

6 lettuce leaves

6 slices cooked deli
  chicken or turkey
  (about 6 ounces)

4 cherry tomatoes

4 pickle chunks

## TOOLS YOU NEED

• Measuring cups
• Small bowl
• Rubber spatula
• Measuring spoons
• Wooden spoon
• Paper towels
• Large microwavable
  plate
• Pot holders
• Cutting board
• Sharp knife
• Toaster or toaster
  oven
• Table knife
• 4 wooden skewers
  (each 10 inches long)

1 Measure out the mayonnaise. Put it in the bowl. Use the rubber spatula to scrape it all out of the measuring cup. Measure out the Thousand Island salad dressing. Add it to the bowl. Mix them all together with the wooden spoon.

2 Put a paper towel on the plate. Lay the slices of bacon across the paper towel. Cover the bacon with another paper towel. Microwave the bacon on High 5 to 6 minutes, until crisp. Carefully take the plate out of the microwave with the pot holders. Set the plate aside so the bacon cools.

3 Wash the tomato. Put it on its side on the cutting board. Use the sharp knife to cut it into 6 slices.

4 Toast the slices of bread in the toaster or toaster oven. Use the table knife to spread the mayonnaise mixture onto 1 side of each slice of the toasted bread.

5 Put 3 slices of toasted bread, spread side up, on the kitchen counter. Put 1 lettuce leaf and 2 slices of chicken on top of each these slices of bread. Then put 3 more slices of bread, spread side down, on top of the chicken. Top each of these slices of bread with 1 lettuce leaf, 2 tomato slices and 2 crisp bacon slices. Cover the bacon with the last 3 slices of bread, spread side down.

6 Put the sandwiches on the cutting board. Use the sharp knife to cut each sandwich diagonally into 4 pieces.

7 Take 1 of the wooden skewers and stick the food on the skewer in this order:
  1 Sandwich piece
  1 Cherry tomato
  1 Sandwich piece
  1 Pickle chunk
  1 Sandwich piece

*1 Sandwich: Calories 420; Total Fat 24g; Sodium 740mg; Total Carbohydrates 32g (Sugars 5g); Protein 21g • Exchanges: 2 Starch, 2 Lean Meat*

### SKY-HIGH SANDWICH
The sky's the limit when it comes to toppings for these sandwich kabobs. You can add slices of your favorite cheese, slices of onion, bell peppers and different deli meat if you like. Just remember the sandwich has to fit in your mouth.

# Bacon and Egg Pita Pockets

TIME IT TAKES: 40 minutes • HOW MUCH IT MAKES: 4 pita pockets

## INGREDIENTS

6 eggs

1/3 cup Alfredo sauce (from a jar or container)

1/4 cup real bacon pieces

1/8 teaspoon onion powder

1 tablespoon chopped fresh parsley

Dash of pepper

2 pita (pocket) breads (each 6 inches in diameter)

## TOOLS YOU NEED

- Medium saucepan with lid (2 quart)
- Table knife
- Cutting board
- Medium bowl
- Measuring cups
- Measuring spoons
- Paper towel
- Kitchen scissors
- Wooden spoon
- Sharp knife
- Spoon
- Microwavable plastic wrap or waxed paper

1   Put the eggs in the saucepan and add enough water to cover the eggs so the tops of the eggs are 1 inch below the top of the water. Put the saucepan on top of the stove and turn the heat to medium-high. When the water boils, take the saucepan off the heat and put the cover on top. Let the covered saucepan stand for 18 minutes. Then take off the cover and put the saucepan in the sink. Run cold water over the eggs until they don't feel warm anymore.

2   Take the eggs out of the cold water and lightly tap the egg on a tabletop or other hard surface to crack the shell all over. Then roll the egg between your hands to loosen the shell. Starting at the large end of the egg, peel off the shell. Use the table knife to chop the eggs into bite-size pieces on the cutting board. Put the chopped eggs in the bowl.

3   Measure out the Alfredo sauce and the bacon pieces. Put them in the bowl. Measure out the onion powder. Add it to the bowl, too.

4   Rinse about 2 handfuls of parsley with cold water. Pat it dry with a paper towel. Use the kitchen scissors to snip the leafy part of the parsley into little pieces. Measure out 1 tablespoon. Toss the parsley into the bowl. Sprinkle a little pepper into the bowl, too. Mix it all up with the wooden spoon.

5   Use the sharp knife to cut each pita bread in half on the cutting board. You should now have 4 halves. Open the halves to make pockets. Spoon the egg mixture into each of the pockets.

6   Wrap each pocket sandwich loosely in plastic wrap or waxed paper. Microwave each sandwich on High 20 to 30 seconds, until warm. Be careful when you take the plastic wrap off the sandwiches because hot steam may come out.

*1 Pita Pocket: Calories 280; Total Fat 17g; Sodium 400mg; Total Carbohydrates 17g (Sugars 1g); Protein 15g • Exchanges: 1 Starch, 2 Fat*

**SAFETY FIRST!**
If you're not going to eat the pocket sandwiches right away, be sure to store the bacon and the egg salad mixture in the bowl covered with plastic wrap in the refrigerator.

# Taco Scoopers

TIME IT TAKES: 20 minutes • HOW MUCH IT MAKES: 2 servings
(1/2 cup dip and 1 cup chips each)

## INGREDIENTS

1/2 cup bean dip (from a can)

1/4 cup chive and onion sour cream

1/4 cup chopped ripe olives

1/4 of a medium tomato

1/4 cup shredded Mexican cheese blend (1 ounce)

2 cups (2 ounces) large corn chips

## TOOLS YOU NEED

• Measuring cups
• Spoon
• 2 small bowls
• (3/4 to 1 cup each)
• Sharp knife
• Cutting board
• Plastic wrap
• 2 serving plates

1 Measure out the bean dip. Spoon half of the dip into each of the bowls. Use the spoon to smooth out the dip.

2 Measure out the chive and onion sour cream. Spoon half of the sour cream into each of the bowls.

3 Measure out the olives. Spoon half of them into each of the bowls.

4  Use the sharp knife to cut the tomato piece into little pieces on the cutting board. Spoon half of the tomato pieces into each of the bowls.

5 Measure out the cheese. (See the How-To Photo.) Spoon half of the cheese into each of the bowls. Cover the bowls tightly with plastic wrap. Put the bowls in the refrigerator until you are ready to eat.

6 When you're ready to eat, divide the chips equally onto 2 plates. Take the plastic wrap off the bowls of dip and put 1 bowl on each plate. To eat, scoop up the dip with the chips.

*1 Serving:* Calories 350; Total Fat 25g; Sodium 820mg; Total Carbohydrates 27g (Sugars 5g); Protein 10g • *Exchanges:* 2 Starch, 4 Fat

### SERVE IT UP
Instead of putting the dip in the small bowls, try layering it on a serving plate. You could get really fancy and add some shredded lettuce after the sour cream and before the olives.

# Chicken Lickin' Lunch Combo

TIME IT TAKES: 20 minutes • HOW MUCH IT MAKES: 1 lunch

## INGREDIENTS

1 medium stalk celery

8 to 10 ready-to-eat
baby-cut carrots

5 large round wheat
crackers

1 can (3 ounces) water-
packed chunk
chicken breast (from
a 3-pack box)

1 container (2.5
ounces) ranch salad
dressing (from a
6-pack box)

1 apple

## TOOLS YOU NEED

• Sharp knife
• Cutting board
• Plastic container
  with lid (1 cup)
• Insulated lunch bag
• 2 resealable food-
  storage plastic bags
  (sandwich size)
• Plastic fork
• Plastic spoon

1   Wash the celery. Use the sharp knife to cut it into very small pieces on the cutting board. Put the celery pieces in the plastic container. Put the lid on and seal it tightly. Put it in the insulated lunch bag.

2   Put the baby carrots in a plastic bag and seal it tightly. Put the crackers in the other plastic bag and seal it, too.

3   Add the can of chicken, the container of salad dressing, the apple, the bag of carrots and the bag of crackers to the lunch bag. Don't forget to add the plastic fork and spoon.

4   At lunch time, open the can of chicken and the container of salad dressing. Use the fork to lift the chicken from the can, leaving the liquid in the can. Add the drained chicken and the salad dressing to the container with the celery. Mix it up with the spoon.

5   To eat, spoon the chicken mixture onto the crackers. The carrots and the apple complete the lunch.

*1 Lunch: Calories 580; Total Fat 38g; Sodium 1,150mg; Total Carbohydrates 46g (Sugars 31g); Protein 18g • Exchanges: 1 Fruit, 1 Vegetable, 2 Very Lean Meat, 7 Fat*

**HATS OFF TO HEALTH!**
Baby-cut carrots are a good thing to pack in your lunch because they're high in Vitamin A (a vitamin that's good for your eyes). They also help you get your recommended 5 servings of fruits and veggies a day.

# Cheesy Beef and Pickle Roll-Ups

TIME IT TAKES: 20 minutes • HOW MUCH IT MAKES: 4 roll-ups

## INGREDIENTS

6 tablespoons process
  cheese spread with
  bacon (from a jar)
4 slices cooked roast
  beef (1/8 inch thick)
12 baby dill pickles,
  well drained
Ketchup and/or
  mustard,
  if desired

## TOOLS YOU NEED

• Measuring spoons
• Custard cup
• Rubber spatula
• Table knife
• Paper towel
• Sharp knife
• Cutting board

1 Measure out the cheese spread. Put it in the custard cup. Scrape all of it out of the measuring spoon with the rubber spatula.

2 Lay the roast beef slices on the kitchen counter. Use the table knife to spread the cheese spread on each slice.

3 Count out 12 pickles. Put them on a paper towel to drain off the juice. Lay 3 pickles across 1 of the short sides of each slice of roast beef. If the pickles don't fit, trim them with the table knife.

4 Roll up the roast beef slices. Use the sharp knife to cut each roll crosswise into 1-inch chunks on the cutting board. To eat, dip the roll-ups in ketchup or mustard.

*1 Roll-Up: Calories 180; Total Fat 11g; Sodium 1,750mg; Total Carbohydrates 7g (Sugars 5g); Protein 15g • Exchanges: 2 Medium-Fat Meat*

### HAM IT UP
If you like, you can use slices of ham instead of roast beef and substitute slices of American cheese for the cheese spread. It's totally up to you!

# Silly Snake Dogs

**TIME IT TAKES:** 45 minutes • **HOW MUCH IT MAKES:** 6 snake dogs

## INGREDIENTS

Piece of red bell
  pepper
1 can (11 ounces)
  refrigerated
  breadsticks
6 hot dogs with
  cheese
1/2 teaspoon sharp
  Cheddar process
  cheese spread (from
  a jar)
12 dried currants

## TOOLS YOU NEED

- Kitchen scissors
- Foil
- Ruler
- Sharp knife
- Cutting board
- Cookie sheet
- Pot holders
- Pancake turner
- Serving tray
- Measuring spoons

1  Heat the oven to 375°F. Use the kitchen scissors to cut out 12 squares of foil that are 3 inches long and 3 inches wide. Loosely crumple each square of foil into a small ball. Then cut out 6 squares of foil that are 2 inches long and 2 inches wide. Shape each of these squares into a tiny ball.

2  Use the sharp knife to cut 6 tiny strips shaped like a tongue from the piece of red bell pepper on the cutting board.

3  Remove the dough from the can, but do not unroll it. Separate the dough into 6 rolls where it wants to come apart.

4  To make each snake, unroll 1 roll of dough. Press to seal the center perforation so you wind up with 1 long breadstick. (Perforations are tiny cuts in the dough that look like lines.) Loosely wrap the long breadstick around 1 hot dog, leaving about 1 1/2 inches of dough at each end that is not wrapped. Put the breadstick-wrapped hot dog on the cookie sheet, seam side down. (You do not need to grease the cookie sheet.) Pinch the dough at 1 end into a rounded point to form the head of the snake. Do this with all the breadsticks and hot dogs.

5  Put 1 small ball of foil at each end of the dough-wrapped hot dogs, propping the "heads" and "tails" up on the balls so they stand up when they're baked. (See the How-To Photo.)

6  Use the kitchen scissors to cut a 1/2-inch slit in the tip of each "head" to form a mouth. Prop each "mouth" open with a tiny ball of foil.

7  Bake the snake dogs for 14 to 17 minutes or until they look deep golden brown.

8  Carefully take the cookie sheet out of the oven with the pot holders. Use the pancake turner to remove the snake dogs from the cookie sheet and put them on the tray. Remove the foil balls. Measure out the cheese spread. Use a little bit of the cheese spread to attach the currants to each "head" to make the eyes. Do the same thing to attach the bell pepper "tongue" in each "mouth." Serve them while they are warm.

*1 Snake Dog: Calories 290; Total Fat 16g; Sodium 910mg; Total Carbohydrates 29g (Sugars 6g); Protein 9g • Exchanges: 2 Starch, 2 Fat*

# Shake-It-Up Salad

**TIME IT TAKES: 15 minutes • HOW MUCH IT MAKES: 1 salad**

## INGREDIENTS

2 tablespoons French
salad dressing

1/4 cup cubed cooked
chicken (1 ounce)

2 tablespoons
shredded Cheddar
cheese

1/2 of a small carrot

1 cup torn prewashed
salad greens

## TOOLS YOU NEED

- Measuring spoons
- Plastic container
  with tight-fitting lid
  (1 quart)
- Rubber spatula
- Measuring cups
- Waxed paper
- Grater

1   Measure out the salad dressing. Put it in the plastic container. Scrape all the salad dressing out of the measuring spoon with the rubber spatula.

2   Measure out the cooked chicken. Toss it into the container on top of the salad dressing.

3   Measure out the Cheddar cheese. Toss it into the container on top of the chicken.

4   Put a piece of waxed paper on the counter. Wash the carrot. Take the carrot and rub it up and down on the grater over the waxed paper. Then measure out 2 tablespoons of the shredded carrot. Toss the carrot shreds into the container on top of the cheese.

5   Measure out the salad greens. Toss them into the container on top of the carrot shreds. Cover the plastic container tightly with the lid. Put it in the refrigerator.

6   When you're ready to eat, shake the container up and down to toss the salad.

*1 Salad: Calories 240; Total Fat 17g; Sodium 520mg; Total Carbohydrates 11g (Sugars 8g); Protein 13g • Exchanges: 2 Lean Meat, 2 Fat*

### SHORT CUT
Instead of using the grater to shred the carrots yourself, you can buy them already shredded in a bag in the vegetable area at the grocery store.

Tea

# Party

Fancy food for
pretty plates

# Teapot Cake with Tea-Cupcakes

TIME IT TAKES: 1 hour 40 minutes • HOW MUCH IT MAKES: 14 servings

## INGREDIENTS

Shortening

1 box (18.25 ounces) yellow cake mix with pudding

1 1/4 cups water

1/3 cup vegetable oil

3 eggs

2 cups vanilla ready-to-spread frosting (from 2 cans)

7 small flower-shaped butter cookies

Small jelly beans

1 sugar ice cream cone (one with a point)

Green chewy fruit snack roll

## TOOLS YOU NEED

• Paper towel
• 2 similar-shaped oven-proof bowls (1 quart each)
• Medium muffin pan (with 12 cups in it)
• Large bowl
• Liquid measuring cup (1 cup)
• Electric mixer
• Rubber spatula
• Measuring cups
• Spoon

(continued on next page)

1 Heat the oven to 350ºF.

2 Use a paper towel to spread a little bit of shortening on the inside of the 2 ovenproof bowls. Put shortening on the inside of 10 of the cups in the muffin pan, too.

3 Put the cake mix in the large bowl. Measure out the water in the liquid measuring cup. Pour it into the bowl. Measure out the oil in the same cup. Pour it into the bowl, too. Crack 1 of the eggs on the edge of the bowl. Open the shell, letting the egg slide into the bowl. Do the same thing with the other 2 eggs. Use the electric mixer on low speed to beat everything in the bowl for 30 seconds. Then beat on medium speed for 2 minutes, scraping the inside edges of the bowl every once in a while with the rubber spatula.

4 Measure out 1 3/4 cups of batter. Pour it into 1 of the ovenproof bowls. Put the same amount of batter in the other bowl. Spoon the batter that's left equally into the 10 muffin cups. The cups should be a little more than halfway full.

5 Put the bowls of cake batter in the oven first. Then put the muffin pan in the oven. Bake 13 to 18 minutes or until a toothpick you stick in the center of a cupcake comes out without any batter on it. Be careful when you stick the toothpick in so that you don't touch the hot oven. Carefully take ONLY the muffin pan out of the oven with the pot holders. Leave the bowls of cake batter in the oven and shut the oven door. Put the muffin pan on a wire rack. Let it cool for 10 minutes.

6 Continue baking the bowl cakes for another 12 to 27 minutes or until a toothpick you stick into the center of each of the bowl cake comes out without any batter on it. Carefully take the bowls out of the oven with the pot holders. Put each of them on a wire rack. Let them cool for 10 minutes.

7 While the bowl cakes are baking, take the cupcakes out of the muffin pan. Put them on the wire rack. Let them cool for 20 minutes or until they aren't warm when you touch them.

8 When the cakes in the bowls have cooled for 10 minutes, take them out of the bowls. Put them on wire racks. Let these cakes cool for 20 minutes or until they aren't warm when you touch them.

9 Put each cupcake on a saucer. Measure out the frosting. Use the table knife to spread some of the frosting on the side and top of each cupcake. Break 5 butter cookies in half. Press half a butter cookie into the side of each cupcake for a handle. Put some jelly beans in a flower shape on the side of each cupcake.

*(continued from previous page)*
- Toothpicks
- Pot holders
- Wire cooling racks
- 10 saucers
- Table knife
- Serrated knife
- Large serving plate (10 inch)
- Cutting board

**10** Use the serrated knife to cut off the tops of the bowl cakes to make that side flat. (See the How-To Photo.) Put 1 of the trimmed-off cake tops aside to use later as the teapot lid. Use the table knife to spread a little of the frosting that's left on the flat side of each bowl cake. Stick the 2 frosted sides of the bowl cakes together so it looks like a round teapot. Put the "teapot" on the plate.

**11** Use the serrated knife to cut 1 inch off the pointy end of the ice cream cone on the cutting board. Throw away the point or eat it. Press the wide end of the cone that's left into the side of the "teapot" so it looks like a spout. Use the table knife to spread some of the frosting that's left all over the "teapot" and "spout." Put the cake top that you set aside earlier on top of the frosted teapot for the lid. Spread the rest of the frosting on the "lid."

**12** Place 1 jelly bean on top of the "lid" for the handle. Press 2 cookies into 1 side of the "teapot" for a handle. Make a few jelly-bean flowers on the sides of "teapot" to match the "teacups." Use the sharp knife to cut some leaf and stem shapes from the fruit snack roll on the cutting board. Put them next to the flowers on the "teacups" and "teapot."

*1 Serving: Calories 350; Total Fat 13g; Sodium 170mg; Total Carbohydrates 55g (Sugars 46g); Protein 2g • Exchanges: 3 Fat*

# Sunflower Sandwiches

**TIME IT TAKES: 60 minutes • HOW MUCH IT MAKES: 8 sandwiches**

## INGREDIENTS

### BISCUITS

1 can (16.3 ounces) large refrigerated original or buttermilk flaky biscuits

1 egg

4 teaspoons sunflower nuts

### TOPPINGS

1 large tomato

8 small lettuce leaves

8 slices (3/4 ounce each) American cheese

4 ounces thinly sliced cooked ham

## TOOLS YOU NEED

• 2 cookie sheets
• Ruler
• Kitchen scissors
• Custard cup
• Fork
• Pastry brush
• Pot holders
• Pancake turner
• Wire cooling racks
• Cutting board
• Sharp knife
• Paper towels

**1** Heat the oven to 350ºF.

**2** Remove the dough from the can. Separate it into 8 biscuits. Use your fingers to split each biscuit in half from side to side to make 2 round halves. Put 8 biscuit halves on each cookie sheet. They should not touch each other and should be about 2 inches apart. Use your fingers to press out each biscuit half to make it about 3 1/2 inches across—use a ruler if you want to.

**3** Bake the biscuit halves on the cookie sheet for 12 minutes or until they look golden brown. While the first cookie sheet is in the oven, press out the other 8 biscuit halves on the second cookie sheet just like you did before. Use the kitchen scissors to make short cuts around the edges of these biscuit halves to look like petals.

**4** Crack the egg on the edge of the custard cup. Open the shell, letting the egg slide into the cup. Beat the egg with the fork. Use the pastry brush to brush beaten egg on the center of each flower shape. Sprinkle 1/2 teaspoon sunflower nuts onto the beaten egg on each biscuit half.

**5** Carefully take the first cookie sheet out of the oven with the pot holders. Put the second cookie sheet in the oven. Bake these halves for 12 minutes or until they look golden brown, too. Use the pancake turner to remove the biscuit halves from the first cookie sheet and put them on the wire racks to cool.

**6** While the second cookie sheet is in the oven, wash the tomato. Put it on its side on the cutting board. Use the sharp knife to cut it into thin slices.

**7** Carefully take the second cookie sheet out of the oven with the pot holders. Use the pancake turner to remove the biscuit halves from this cookie sheet and place them on the wire racks with the other biscuit halves to cool.

**8** Wash the lettuce leaves. Pat them dry with paper towels. To make the sandwiches, arrange 1 lettuce leaf, 1 slice of cheese, 1 slice of ham and 1 tomato slice on each plain biscuit half. Top each sandwich with the other biscuit half, sunflower nut side up.

*1 Sandwich: Calories 330; Total Fat 18g; Sodium 1,230mg; Total Carbohydrates 29g (Sugars 9g); Protein 13g • Exchanges: 2 Starch, 1 High-Fat Meat, 2 Fat*

# Sweetly Spiced Party Tea

TIME IT TAKES: 15 minutes • HOW MUCH IT MAKES: 10 cups of tea (²/₃ cup each)

## INGREDIENTS

6 cups water

5 cinnamon-apple
spice herbal tea bags

1 can (6 ounces) frozen
orange juice
concentrate

1/2 cup honey

## TOOLS YOU NEED

• Liquid measuring
cup (1 cup)
• Large saucepan
• Slotted spoon
• Rubber spatula
• Teapot
• Tea cups

**1** Measure out the water in the liquid measuring cup. Pour it into the saucepan. Heat the water over medium-high heat until it bubbles. Remove the saucepan from the hot burner. Toss in the tea bags. Let the tea bags sit in the hot water for 5 minutes.

**2** Use the slotted spoon to carefully take the tea bags out of the hot water. You can throw them away. Add the orange juice concentrate to the hot water. Stir it up with the spoon.

**3** Measure out the honey in the liquid measuring cup. Pour it into the saucepan. Scrape it all out of the measuring cup with the rubber spatula. Stir everything together so it's all mixed up. Pour the tea into the teapot. Serve the warm tea in the teacups.

*1 Cup of Tea:* Calories 80; Total Fat 0g; Sodium 0mg; Total Carbohydrates 21g (Sugars 20g); Protein 0g • *Exchanges:* 1 Fruit

### SPECIAL TOUCH
To make the tea look extra nice, cut an orange into slices and then into wedges with a sharp knife on a cutting board. Float 1 wedge of orange in each cup of tea.

Come &

# Get It!

## Scrumptious suppers and side dishes

# Bow Tie Pasta and Peas

TIME IT TAKES: 40 minutes • HOW MUCH IT MAKES: 4 servings (1 cup each)

## INGREDIENTS

3 cups uncooked bow
tie pasta (6 ounces)

1 1/2 cups frozen baby
sweet peas

1 cup Alfredo sauce
(from a jar)

1/2 cup real bacon
pieces

## TOOLS YOU NEED

• Large saucepan
(4 quart)
• Measuring cups
• Wooden spoon
• Colander

1  Fill the saucepan about half full with water. Heat the water over medium-high heat until it is boiling.

2  Measure out the pasta. Pour it into the boiling water. Be careful the very hot water doesn't splash out when you put the pasta in. Let the water start boiling again. Cook the pasta for 6 minutes. Stir the pasta every once in a while with the wooden spoon.

3  Measure out the peas. When the 6 minutes are up, add the peas to the boiling water. Let the water start boiling again. Cook the pasta and peas for another 4 minutes. Stir them every once in a while with the wooden spoon.

4  Put the colander in the sink. Pour the water, pasta and peas into the colander. Be careful! The steam from the boiling water will be very hot. Shake the colander a few times to drain out as much water out as you can. Then pour the pasta and the peas back into the saucepan.

5  Measure out the Alfredo sauce and the bacon pieces. Add them to the pasta and peas in the saucepan. Use the wooden spoon to mix it all up.

6  Heat the pasta mixture over low heat, stirring with the wooden spoon, until everything in the saucepan is heated all the way through.

*1 Serving: Calories 450; Total Fat 25g; Sodium 460mg; Total Carbohydrates 44g (Sugars 5g); Protein 16g • Exchanges: 1 Vegetable, 1 High-Fat Meat, 3 Fat*

### PASTA POWER

There are lots of different pasta shapes to choose from. You might want to try making this dish with penne, wagon wheels or rotini instead of bow tie pasta. Because some sizes of pasta take longer to cook than others, remember to follow the cooking directions on the package of whatever kind of pasta you choose.

# Funny Face-Topped Chowder

**TIME IT TAKES: 40 minutes • HOW MUCH IT MAKES: 4 servings (1 1/4 cups each)**

## INGREDIENTS

6 ounces cooked ham
(1 cup)

1 cup frozen whole
kernel corn

1/2 cup shoestring
potatoes

8 small pimiento-
stuffed olives

1 cherry tomato

2 cans (18.5 ounces
each) ready-to-serve
potato with broccoli
and cheese chowder

## TOOLS YOU NEED

• Sharp knife
• Cutting board
• Measuring cups
• Large saucepan
with lid
• Can opener
• Wooden spoon
• Hot pad
• Ladle
• 4 soup bowls

**1** Use the sharp knife to cut the ham into little pieces on the cutting board. Measure out 1 cup. Put the ham in the large saucepan. Measure out the corn. Put it in the saucepan, too.

**2** Measure out the shoestring potatoes. Count out 8 olives. Wash the cherry tomato. Use the sharp knife to cut it into 4 wedges on the cutting board. Set the shoestring potatoes, olives and tomato aside. You'll use them later.

**3** Open the cans of soup with the can opener. Pour the soup into the saucepan. Use the wooden spoon to mix it all up.

**4** Heat the mixture over medium-high heat until it begins to boil. Turn the heat down to medium. Heat the soup for 10 minutes. Stir the mixture every once in a while with the wooden spoon to keep it from sticking to the bottom of the saucepan.

**5** Take the saucepan off the hot burner. Set it on the hot pad on the kitchen counter. Use the ladle to put the soup into the 4 bowls. Put 2 olives on the soup in each bowl to look like eyes. Arrange the tomato quarters under the "eyes" for the mouths. Put a few shoestring potatoes around the edge of each bowl to look like hair or beard.

*1 Serving: Calories 340; Total Fat 19g; Sodium 1,770mg; Total Carbohydrates 26g (Sugars 5g); Protein 19g • Exchanges: 2 Very Lean Meat*

## ON THE SIDE
If you like, you can toast up some bread to serve with this cheesy chowder. A cold glass of milk would also taste great.

# Easy Tostada Pizzas

**TIME IT TAKES: 45 minutes • HOW MUCH IT MAKES: 4 pizzas**

## INGREDIENTS

1 package (9 ounces)
  frozen southwestern-
  seasoned cooked
  chicken breast strips

1 cup shredded
  Mexican cheese
  blend (4 ounces)

1/2 cup thick 'n
  chunky salsa

1 can (11.5 ounces)
  refrigerated
  cornbread twists

## TOOLS YOU NEED

• Large microwavable
  plate
• Measuring cups
• Small bowl or dish
• Rubber spatula
• Spoon
• Cookie sheet
• Ruler
• Pot holders
• Pancake turner
• 4 serving plates

1  Heat the oven to 375ºF.

2  Put the frozen chicken strips on the microwavable plate. Microwave the chicken on Low 2 to 3 minutes, until thawed. Take the plate of chicken out of the microwave.

3  Measure out the cheese. Set it aside. Measure out the salsa. Put it in the bowl or dish. Scrape all the salsa out of the measuring cup with the rubber spatula. Put the spoon in the salsa. Set that aside, too. You'll need the cheese and the salsa later.

4  Remove the dough from the can. Unroll the dough and separate it into 4 rectangles. Each rectangle should be made of 4 strips. Carefully lay the rectangles on the cookie sheet. (You do not need to grease the cookie sheet.) Press each rectangle out with your fingers until it is 5 1/2 long and 4 1/2 inches wide.

5  Divide the thawed chicken strips into 4 equal piles. Put 1 pile of chicken strips on each rectangle. Sprinkle cheese on top of each of the piles of chicken.

6  Bake the pizzas for 15 to 20 minutes or until the edges look deep golden brown. Carefully take the cookie sheet out of the oven with the pot holders. Use the pancake turner to remove the pizzas from the cookie sheet and put them on the plates. Serve the pizzas with the salsa.

*1 Pizza: Calories 480; Total Fat 23g; Sodium 1,260mg; Total Carbohydrates 36g (Sugars 9g); Protein 33g • Exchanges: 2 Fat*

**MAKE IT MEXICAN**
To add even more South-of-the-border flavor, serve these mini pizzas with tortilla chips and refried beans. Olé!

# Zesty Fish Stick Tacos

**TIME IT TAKES:** 30 minutes • **HOW MUCH IT MAKES:** 6 servings (2 tacos each)

## INGREDIENTS

24 frozen fish sticks

3/4 cup mayonnaise

2 tablespoons taco
seasoning mix (from
a package)

1 medium tomato

1 1/2 cups chopped
lettuce (from a bag)

1 box (10.5 ounces)
flour tortillas for soft
tacos and fajitas
(12 tortillas)

Taco sauce, if desired

## TOOLS YOU NEED

• Measuring cups
• Measuring spoons
• Medium bowl
• Rubber spatula
• Wooden spoon
• Cookie sheet
• Sharp knife
• Cutting board
• Microwavable plates
• Microwavable plastic
  wrap
• Pot holders
• Pancake turner
• Table knife

1 Heat the oven as directed on the box of fish sticks.

2 Measure out the mayonnaise. Use the rubber spatula to scrape all of it out of the measuring cup into the bowl. Measure out the taco seasoning mix. Put it in the bowl. Mix them up with the wooden spoon.

3 Put the fish sticks on the cookie sheet. Bake them as directed on the box. While the fish sticks are baking, wash the tomato. Use the sharp knife to cut it into small pieces on the cutting board. Measure out the lettuce.

4 Remove the tortillas from the box. Stack them on the plate. Cover the tortillas with a piece of plastic wrap. Microwave the tortillas on High 1 minute.

5 When the fish sticks are done baking, carefully take the cookie sheet out of the oven with the pot holders. Use the pancake turner to remove the fish sticks from the cookie sheet and put them on the cutting board. Use the table knife to cut each warm fish stick into 4 pieces.

6 Divide the mayonnaise mixture evenly onto the tortillas. Use the table knife to spread the mixture over the tortilla. Top 1 side of each tortilla with 8 fish stick pieces, a little of the lettuce and some of the tomato. Fold the side of each tortilla without the toppings over the top. Serve the tacos with taco sauce.

*2 Tacos: Calories 570; Total Fat 36g; Sodium 810mg; Total Carbohydrates 48g (Sugars 7g); Protein 14g • Exchanges: 3 Starch, 6 Fat*

### GO FISH
Instead of making fish stick tacos, try making fish stick sandwiches. Just use hamburger buns instead of the flour tortillas.

# Hot Diggity Dog Pizza Boats

TIME IT TAKES: 15 minutes • HOW MUCH IT MAKES: 4 pizza boats

## INGREDIENTS

4 hot dogs

2 tablespoons sliced green olives

1 can (8 ounces) pizza sauce

4 hot dog buns

1/2 cup shredded pizza cheese blend (2 ounces)

## TOOLS YOU NEED

• Table knife
• Cutting board
• Measuring spoons
• Medium saucepan (2 quart)
• Measuring cups
• Can opener
• Wooden spoon
• Serrated knife
• Hot pad
• Spoon

1   Use the table knife to cut the hot dogs into slices on the cutting board. Measure out the olives. Put the hot dog slices and the olives in the saucepan. Measure out the cheese. Set it aside. You'll use it later.

2   Open the can of pizza sauce with the can opener. Pour the pizza sauce into the saucepan. Mix it all up with the wooden spoon.

3   Cook the hot dogs, olives and pizza sauce over medium heat for 4 to 5 minutes, until everything is hot. Stir the mixture every once in a while with the wooden spoon so it doesn't stick to the bottom of the saucepan.

4   If the hot dog buns aren't already split down the middle, use the serrated knife to cut them almost in half on the cutting board. Remove the saucepan from the hot burner. Set it on the hot pad on the kitchen counter. Spoon the mixture from the saucepan into the hot dog buns. Sprinkle some cheese over the top of each pizza boat.

*1 Pizza Boat:* Calories 350; Total Fat 22g; Sodium 1,240mg; Total Carbohydrates 28g (Sugars 8g); Protein 13g • *Exchanges:* 2 Starch, 1 High-Fat Meat, 2 Fat

**EXTRA CREDIT**
To make the cheese on these pizza boats even more ooey and gooey, put the boats on a cookie sheet and put the cookie sheet under the broiler for 2 to 3 minutes. Remember to use pot holders when removing!

# Grilled Cheese-Tomato Soup

TIME IT TAKES: 10 minutes  •  HOW MUCH IT MAKES: 2 servings (1 1/4 cups each)

## INGREDIENTS

1 can (19 ounces)
  ready-to-serve
  tomato basil soup

1/2 cup croutons

2 individual-size bags
  (1.5 ounces each)
  Colby-Monterey Jack
  cheese blend cubes

## TOOLS YOU NEED

- Can opener
- Medium saucepan
- Wooden spoon
- Measuring cups
- 2 resealable food-
  storage plastic bags
  (sandwich size)
- 2 insulated bottles
- 2 plastic spoons
- 2 lunch bags

1   Open the can of soup with the can opener. Pour the soup into the saucepan. Heat the soup over medium heat until it is hot. Stir every once in a while with the wooden spoon.

2   While the soup is heating, measure out the croutons. Divide them equally into the 2 plastic bags.

3   Carefully pour the warm soup into the 2 insulated bottles, dividing it equally. Pack 1 bottle of soup, 1 plastic bag of croutons, 1 bag of cheese cubes and 1 plastic spoon in each of the 2 lunch bags.

4   At lunch time, drop the cheese cubes and the croutons into the warm soup.

*1 Serving: Calories 300; Total Fat 16g; Sodium 1,400mg; Total Carbohydrates 26g (Sugars 9g); Protein 13g • Exchanges: Free*

**TOP THIS!**
If you want, you can sprinkle shredded cheese in this scrumptious tomato soup instead of using the cheese cubes. Tiny fish-shaped crackers also taste good.

# Italian Beef Dippers

TIME IT TAKES: 30 minutes • HOW MUCH IT MAKES: 6 servings
(1 sandwich and 1/3 cup soup each)

## INGREDIENTS

1 can (18.5 ounces)
   ready-to-serve
   French onion soup

1/2 teaspoon dried
   Italian seasoning

3/4 pound thinly sliced
   Italian- or garlic-
   seasoned cooked
   roast beef

6 crusty French rolls
   (each 3 to 4 inches
   long)

6 slices (3/4 ounce
   each) provolone
   cheese

## TOOLS YOU NEED

• Can opener
• Medium saucepan
   (2 quart)
• Measuring spoons
• Wooden spoon
• Serrated knife
• Cutting board
• Slotted spoon
• Table knife
• Measuring cups
• 6 custard cups

1  Open the can of soup with the can opener. Pour the soup into the saucepan. Measure out the Italian seasoning. Toss it in the saucepan. Mix up the soup and the seasoning with the wooden spoon.

2  Heat the soup over medium heat until it is hot. Stir the soup every once in a while with the wooden spoon. Add the slices of beef to the soup. Continue to heat the soup and the beef for 4 to 6 minutes, until they are heated all the way through. Stir the soup and beef every once in a while with the wooden spoon so it doesn't stick to the bottom of the saucepan.

3  Use the serrated knife to cut the French rolls in half sideways on the cutting board. Use the slotted spoon to remove the slices of beef from the soup. Put the beef on the bottom halves of the rolls. If you like onions, put a few onions from the soup on the beef.

4  Cut each slice of cheese into 2 pieces with the table knife. Put 2 pieces of cheese on top of the beef on each sandwich. Cover the beef and cheese with the top halves of the rolls.

5  Scoop out 1/3 cup soup and put it in 1 of the custard cups. Put the same amount of soup in each of the other custard cups. (If there's any soup left over, divide it into the cups.) Serve the sandwiches with the warm soup for dipping.

*1 Serving:* Calories 280; Total Fat 10g; Sodium 1,410mg; Total Carbohydrates 28g (Sugars 3g); Protein 20g • *Exchanges:* 2 Starch, 2 Very Lean Meat, 1 Fat

**FANCY FOOD**
If you want to sound super smart, you can call this recipe Italian Beef Dippers au Jus. "Au jus" is pronounced "oh zhoo" and it is how French people say "with juice."

# Meatball and Biscuit Kabobs

**TIME IT TAKES:** 40 minutes • **HOW MUCH IT MAKES:** 4 servings
(1 kabob and 1/4 cup sauce each)

## INGREDIENTS

12 frozen cooked
   Italian meatballs

1 can (10.2 ounces)
   homestyle
   refrigerated
   buttermilk biscuits
   (5 biscuits)

2 tablespoons grated
   Parmesan cheese

1 medium bell pepper
   (pick your favorite
   color)

1 cup tomato pasta
   sauce

## TOOLS YOU NEED

- Large microwavable
  plate
- Resealable food-
  storage plastic bag
  (quart size)
- Kitchen scissors
- Cutting board
- Medium bowl
- Measuring spoons
- Wooden spoon
- Sharp knife
- 4 metal skewers
  (10 or 12 inch)
- Pan (15 x 10 x 1 inch)
- Measuring cups
- Small bowl
- Microwave
- 4 custard cups

1   Heat the oven to 375°F.

2   Count out 12 frozen meatballs. Put them on the plate. Put the rest of the meatballs back in the freezer. Microwave the meatballs on Low 2 to 3 minutes, until thawed. Take the plate of meatballs out of the microwave.

3   Remove the dough from the can. Separate it into 5 biscuits. Use the kitchen scissors to cut each biscuit into 4 same-sized pieces on the cutting board. Put the dough pieces in the medium bowl. Measure out the Parmesan cheese. Toss it into the bowl with the dough. Stir the dough pieces with the wooden spoon so they are covered with the cheese.

4   Wash the bell pepper. Use the sharp knife to cut it in half on the cutting board. Cut off the stem on each half and remove all the seeds. Cut each pepper half into 6 pieces.

5   Take 1 of the metal skewers and stick the food on the skewer in this order:

| | |
|---|---|
| Biscuit piece | Biscuit piece |
| Meatball | Bell pepper piece |
| Biscuit piece | Biscuit piece |
| Bell pepper piece | Meatball |
| Biscuit piece | Bell pepper piece |
| Meatball | |

6   Do the same thing with the other 3 skewers. When you're done, each skewer should have 5 biscuit pieces, 3 meatballs and 3 bell pepper pieces on it. Leave a little space on each side of the biscuit pieces because they will puff up when they bake. Put the kabobs in the pan.

7   Bake the kabobs for 14 to 16 minutes or until the biscuit pieces look deep golden brown. Carefully take the pan out of the oven with the pot holders.

8   While the kabobs are baking, measure out the tomato pasta sauce. Put it in the small bowl. Microwave the sauce on High 20 to 30 seconds, until it is warm. Measure out 1/4 cup of the sauce. Pour it into 1 of the custard cups. Put the same amount in each of the other custard cups.

9   To eat, give each person 1 kabob and 1 custard cup of pasta sauce. Slide the foods off of the skewer. Dip them in the warm sauce.

*1 Serving:* Calories 580; Total Fat 29g; Sodium 1,730mg; Total Carbohydrates 57g
(Sugars 17g); Protein 24g • *Exchanges:* 4 Starch, 2 Medium-Fat Meat, 3 Fat

# Skillet Nacho Chili

**TIME IT TAKES: 40 minutes • HOW MUCH IT MAKES: 4 servings**
(1 1/2 cups chili and 1/2 cup chips each)

## INGREDIENTS

1 can (19 ounces)
   ready-to-serve
   hearty tomato soup

1 can (15 ounces) spicy
   chili beans, undrained

1 can (4.5 ounces)
   chopped green chiles

1 cup frozen whole
   kernel corn

1 medium onion

1 pound lean (at least
   80% lean) ground
   beef

2 cups corn chips

1 bag (4 ounces)
   shredded Cheddar
   cheese (1 cup)

## TOOLS YOU NEED

• Can opener
• Measuring cup
• Sharp knife
• Cutting board
• Extra-large nonstick
   skillet (12 inch)
• Wooden spoon
• Small serving bowl
   or basket
• Hot pad
• Ladle
• 4 soup bowls

1  Open the can of soup, the can of chili beans and the can of green chiles with the can opener. Measure out the corn. Set all of these aside. You'll need them later.

2  Peel off the dry, papery skin of the onion. Use the sharp knife to cut the onion in half on the cutting board. Chop the onion into small pieces. Measure out 1/2 cup.

3  Put the ground beef and the 1/2 cup chopped onion in the skillet. Stir with the wooden spoon until the ground beef is broken into small pieces. Cook over medium-high heat for 5 to 7 minutes, stirring a lot until the ground beef is cooked all the way through and all of it looks brown.

4  Pour the soup, the chili beans, the green chiles and the corn into the skillet. Mix it all up with the wooden spoon. Cook it over medium-high heat until everything begins to bubble. Turn the heat down to medium. Cook another 8 to 10 minutes or until the sauce is kind of thick. Stir the mixture every once in a while with the wooden spoon.

5  Measure out the corn chips. Put them in the serving bowl or basket. Take the skillet off the hot burner. Set it on the hot pad on the kitchen counter. Use the ladle to divide the chili into the 4 bowls. Sprinkle the same amount of cheese on top of each serving. Serve the chili with the chips.

*1 Serving:* Calories 600; Total Fat 32g; Sodium 1,750mg; Total Carbohydrates 45g
(Sugars 10g); Protein 37g • *Exchanges:* 3 Starch, 4 Lean Meat, 3 Fat

### TOP IT OFF
There are lots of yummy things you can put on top of this chili. A spoonful of sour cream, a slice of avocado or chopped onion are all delicious ideas.

# Easy Mac 'n Cheese

TIME IT TAKES: 25 minutes • HOW MUCH IT MAKES: 2 servings (1 1/2cup each)

## INGREDIENTS

1 can (14 ounces) fat-free chicken broth with 1/3 less sodium

1 1/2 cups uncooked elbow macaroni (6 ounces)

1 box (10 ounces) frozen broccoli in cheese-flavored sauce in a pouch

3/4 cup shredded Cheddar cheese (3 ounces)

2 tablespoons grated Parmesan cheese

## TOOLS YOU NEED

• Can opener
• Medium saucepan (2 quart)
• Measuring cups
• Wooden spoon
• Scissors
• 2 serving plates

1  Open the can of chicken broth with the can opener. Pour the broth into the saucepan. Heat the broth over medium-high heat until it starts to bubble.

2  While the chicken broth is heating, measure out the macaroni. When the broth starts bubbling, carefully toss the macaroni into the saucepan. Be careful the very hot water doesn't splash out when you put the macaroni in. When the broth starts to bubble again, cook the macaroni for 10 minutes. Stir every once in a while with the wooden spoon so the macaroni doesn't stick to the saucepan. You'll know the macaroni is done when it is soft and there is only a little bit of broth left in the saucepan. Take the saucepan off the hot burner. Do not drain off the broth.

3  While the macaroni is cooking, microwave the broccoli as directed on the box.

4  Measure out the Cheddar cheese. When the macaroni is done, use the scissors to cut the pouch of broccoli open. Add the broccoli with the cheese sauce to the saucepan. Toss in the Cheddar cheese, too. Mix it up gently with the wooden spoon.

5  Put half of the macaroni mixture on 1 plate and half on the other plate. Measure out 1 tablespoon Parmesan cheese. Sprinkle it on top of 1 of the plates of macaroni. Put the same amount of Parmesan cheese on the other plate of macaroni.

*1 Serving: Calories 630; Total Fat 23g; Sodium 1,450mg; Total Carbohydrates 77g (Sugars 9g); Protein 31g • Exchanges: 5 Starch, 1 Vegetable, 2 High-Fat Meat, 1 Fat*

### PASTA PLEASER
This mac-and-cheese recipe calls for elbow macaroni, but you can pick any kind of pasta you like as long as it is close to the same size. Try shells or twirly rotini if you like.

# Do-Ahead Lasagna Logs

TIME IT TAKES: 40 minutes • HOW MUCH IT MAKES: 8 lasagna logs

## INGREDIENTS

8 uncooked lasagna
  noodles

1 egg

1 container (12 ounces)
  low-fat cottage
  cheese

1 cup shredded
  mozzarella cheese
  (4 ounces)

1/4 cup grated
  Parmesan cheese

1/2 teaspoon dried
  basil leaves

2 cups tomato pasta
  sauce (from a jar)

## TOOLS YOU NEED

• Large saucepan
  (4 quart)
• Colander
• 2 wooden spoons
• Medium bowl
• Fork
• Spoon
• Measuring cups
• Measuring spoons
• Table knife
• Plastic wrap
• Microwavable bowl
• Microwavable wax
  paper

1   Fill the saucepan about half full with water. Heat the water over medium-high heat until it is boiling. Put the colander in the sink.

2   Put the lasagna noodles in the boiling water. Be careful the very hot water doesn't splash out when you put the pasta in. Let the water start boiling again. Stir the noodles every once in a while with a wooden spoon.

3   While the noodles are cooking, crack the egg on the edge of the bowl. Open the shell, letting the egg slide into the bowl. Use the fork to mix up the egg a little. Open the container of cottage cheese and put it in the bowl with the mixed-up egg. Use the spoon to get all the cottage cheese out of the container. Measure out the mozzarella cheese and put it in the bowl. Measure out the Parmesan cheese and put it in the bowl. Measure out the basil leaves. (See the How-To Photo.) Put them in the medium bowl, too. Use a wooden spoon to mix it all up.

4   When the noodles are done cooking, pour the water and noodles into the colander. Be careful! The steam from the bowling water will be very hot. Shake the colander a few times to drain out as much water as you can.

5   Put the cooked noodles on the counter. Use the knife to spread each noodle equally with the cheese mixture. Leave some space at the short end of the noodle. Roll up the noodles tightly toward the unfilled end.

6   Wrap each of the lasagna logs with plastic wrap. Put the logs in the refrigerator or the freezer.

7   To cook one lasagna log, take the log out the refrigerator or freezer and remove the plastic wrap. Put it with the seam side down in a microwavable bowl. Cover the bowl with waxed paper.

**MAKE MINE MEAT!**
If you like meat in your lasagna, ask your adult helper to brown 1 pound of ground beef and add it to the tomato pasta sauce.

8 If you refrigerated your lasagna roll, microwave it on High for 1 to 2 minutes or until the cheese starts to melt at the end. Take the bowl out of the microwave and set in on the counter. Carefully take off the waxed paper. Be careful! Hot steam may come out of the bowl. Measure out 1/4 cup pasta sauce and pour it over the lasagna roll. Microwave on High another 20 to 30 seconds, or until it is warm all the way through. If you froze your lasagna roll, microwave it on Low for 1 to 2 minutes first until it is thawed out, then reheat it like the directions say above.

*1 Lasagna Log:* Calories 240; Total Fat 7g; Sodium 620mg; Total Carbohydrates 29g (Sugars 7g); Protein 15g • *Exchanges:* 2 Starch, 1 Very Lean Meat, 1 Fat

# Chicken Wraps

TIME IT TAKES: 45 minutes  •  HOW MUCH IT MAKES: 8 wraps

## INGREDIENTS

### DIPPING SAUCE

1/2 cup sour cream

1/2 cup mayonnaise

### WRAPS

1 envelope (1 ounce) ranch salad dressing mix

2 tablespoons vegetable oil

1 can (16.3 ounces) refrigerated flaky biscuits

1 package (6 ounce) refrigerated fully cooked grilled chicken breast strips

2 tablespoons butter or margarine (from a stick)

## TOOLS YOU NEED

- Cookie sheet
- Cooking spray
- Measuring spoons
- 2 small bowls
- Spoon
- Ruler
- Table knife
- Custard cup
- Pastry brush
- Measuring cups
- Rubber spatula
- Wooden spoon
- Pot holders
- Pancake turner
- Wire cooling rack

1  Heat the oven to 350ºF. Spray the cookie sheet with cooking spray.

2  Measure out 1 tablespoon of the salad dressing mix and put it in a bowl. Measure out the oil and put it in the bowl. Mix them up with the spoon.

3  Remove the dough from the can. Separate the dough into 8 biscuits. Put the biscuits on the cookie sheet. Use your fingers to press each biscuit into a 6-inch oval. Use the spoon to spread about 1 teaspoon of the salad dressing mixture on top of each biscuit.

4  Put about 3 chicken breast strips crosswise on the center of each biscuit. Bring the ends of biscuit ovals up over chicken, overlapping and pinching them to seal. Use the table knife to cut off 2 tablespoons from the stick of butter. Put it in the custard cup. Put the rest of the butter back in the refrigerator. Microwave the butter on High 5 to 10 seconds, until it is melted. Use the pastry brush to brush the dough with the melted butter. Measure out 2 teaspoons of the dry salad dressing mix. Sprinkle it over the tops of the wraps.

5  Bake the chicken wraps for 18 to 22 minutes or until they look light golden brown.

6  While the chicken wraps are baking, measure out the sour cream and put it in a bowl. Scrape all of it out of the measuring cup with the rubber spatula. Measure out the mayonnaise and put it in the bowl. Use the spatula again to scrape all of it out of the cup. Toss the rest of the ranch salad dressing mix in the bowl. Mix it all together with the wooden spoon.

7  Carefully take the cookie sheet out of the oven with the pot holders. Use the pancake turner to remove the chicken wraps from the cookie sheet and put them on the wire rack to cool. Serve the chicken wraps with the sauce for dipping.

*1 Wrap: Calories 430; Total Fat 29g; Sodium 1,140mg; Total Carbohydrates 30g (Sugars 10g); Protein 12g • Exchanges: 2 Starch, 1 Very Lean Meat*

### SPICE IT UP!

If you want to try an experiment, use taco seasoning mix instead of the ranch salad dressing mix. Salsa would also be a tasty dipping sauce.

# Pepperoni 'n Cheese Crescents

TIME IT TAKES: 40 minutes • HOW MUCH IT MAKES: 4 servings

(2 crescents and 1/4 cup sauce each)

## INGREDIENTS

24 slices pepperoni
  (about 5 ounces)
1/2 cup shredded
  mozzarella cheese
  (2 ounces)
1 can (8 ounces)
  refrigerated crescent
  dinner rolls
1 cup tomato pasta
  sauce or pizza sauce

## TOOLS YOU NEED

• Measuring cups
• Cookie sheet
• Measuring spoons
• Measuring cups
• Small saucepan
  (1 quart)
• Wooden spoon
• Small serving bowl
• Spoon
• Pot holders
• Pancake turner
• Serving platter

1  Heat the oven to 375ºF.

2  Count out 24 slices of pepperoni. Measure out the cheese. Set these aside. You'll use them later.

3  Remove the dough from the can. Unroll it and separate it into 8 triangles. Stretch out each of the triangles a little bit with your fingers.

4  Put 3 pepperoni slices lengthwise down the center of each triangle. It's okay if they touch. Put about 1 tablespoon of cheese on the top of each triangle.

5  Roll up each of the triangles, starting with the shortest side and rolling to the opposite point. Put the rolls, point side down, on the cookie sheet. (You do not need to grease the cookie sheet.)

6  Bake the rolls for 10 to 14 minutes or until they look golden brown.

7  While the rolls are baking, measure out the tomato pasta sauce. Pour it into the saucepan. Heat the sauce over medium-low heat until it is warm. Stir it every once in a while with the wooden spoon. Pour it into the bowl. Add the spoon to the bowl.

8  Carefully take the cookie sheet out of the oven with the pot holders. Use the pancake turner to remove the crescents from the cookie sheet and put them on the platter. Serve the crescents with the pasta sauce for dipping.

*1 Serving:* Calories 480; Total Fat 29g; Sodium 1,790mg; Total Carbohydrates 40g
*(Sugars 14g); Protein 16g •* **Exchanges:** *1 High-Fat Meat, 4 Fat*

> **PIZZA PICK**
> If pepperoni isn't your favorite, try filling these crusty crescents with something different. Cooked sausage, olives and even just cheese would all be mighty tasty.

# Pizza Chicken and Ravioli

**TIME IT TAKES: 30 minutes  •  HOW MUCH IT MAKES: 4 servings (1 1/3 cups each)**

## INGREDIENTS

1 package (9 ounces) refrigerated cheese-filled ravioli

1 jar (2.5 ounces) sliced mushrooms

1 can (14.5 ounces) diced tomatoes with onion and green pepper, undrained

1 can (8 ounces) pizza sauce

1 package (9 ounces) frozen cooked chicken breast strips (2 cups)

## TOOLS YOU NEED

• Large saucepan (4 quart)
• Colander
• Can opener
• Wooden spoon

1  Fill the saucepan about half full with water. Heat the water over medium-high heat until it is boiling. Carefully pour the ravioli into the boiling water. Be careful the very hot water doesn't splash out when you put the ravioli in. Let the water start boiling again. Cook the ravioli as directed on the package.

2  Place the colander in the sink. Pour the water and the ravioli from the saucepan into the colander. Be careful! The steam and the boiling water will be very hot. Put the drained ravioli back into the saucepan.

3  Open the jar of mushrooms. Pour the mushrooms into the colander in the sink so all the juice drains off. Put the drained mushrooms in the saucepan. Open the can of tomatoes and the can of pizza sauce with the can opener. Pour the tomatoes and the pizza sauce into the saucepan.

4  Toss the chicken breast strips into the saucepan. Stir everything up with the wooden spoon. Heat the mixture over medium-high heat for about 5 minutes, stirring a lot, until everything is heated all the way through.

*1 Serving: Calories 290; Total Fat 11g; Sodium 1,390mg; Total Carbohydrates 23g (Sugars 8g); Protein 29g • Exchanges: Free*

**RAVIOLI ROUND UP**
Refrigerated ravioli comes in all sorts of fillings. Check out the selection at your grocery store and pick your favorite kind to use in this recipe.

# Hallowe

# en Party

Scary food to make you scream!

# Monster Burgers

**TIME IT TAKES 45 minutes • HOW MUCH IT MAKES: 8 burgers**

## INGREDIENTS
8 ground beef patties
(4 ounces each)

8 burger buns

8 slices (3/4 ounces
each) American
cheese

8 thin slices cooked
ham

16 slices dill pickle

Ketchup

## TOOLS YOU NEED
• Broiler pan
• Pancake turner
• Serrated knife
• Cutting board
• Serving platter
• Table knife

1    Put the ground beef patties on the broiler pan. Broil the patties 3 to 4 inches from the heat for 5 minutes. Use the pancake turner to flip the patties over. Broil them another 5 to 7 minutes or until they are cooked all they way through.

2    While the ground beef patties are broiling, if the burger buns aren't already in 2 pieces, use the serrated knife to split them in half on the cutting board. Put the bottom halves of the buns on the platter.

3    For each monster burger, use the pancake turner to put 1 cooked patty on the bottom half of the bun. Use the table knife to cut the cheese slice in half in a zigzag pattern to look like teeth. Put half of the cheese slice on the patty, so it looks like the teeth are hanging off 1 side.

4    Take 1 slice of ham and fold it into a tongue shape. Put the ham on top of the "teeth." Put the other half of the cheese on top of the ham. Put the other half of the bun on top of the cheese. Put 2 pickle slices on top of the bun for the eyes. Dot the "eyes" with ketchup.

*1 Burger:* Calories 480; Total Fat 28g; Sodium 1,260mg; Total Carbohydrates 24g (Sugars 7g); Protein 36g • *Exchanges:* 1 Fat

---

**TAKE IT OUTSIDE**
If it's not freezing cold where you live, ask an adult helper to grill the ground beef patties on a gas or charcoal grill instead of broiling them. Then continue with Step 2.

# The Creepiest Salad Bar

TIME IT TAKES: 20 minutes • HOW MUCH IT MAKES: 8 servings

## INGREDIENTS

MONSTER SLIME DRESSING

1 cup ranch salad
   dressing

Green food color

CREEPIEST SALAD STUFF

8 cups spring mix
   lettuce blend
   ("weeds and grass")

24 slices pepperoni
   ("scabs")

1/2 cup sunflower nuts
   ("witches' teeth")

1 cup cherry tomatoes
   ("vampire eyeballs")

1 cup sliced
   mushrooms ("sliced
   toadstools")

1 cup shredded
   mozzarella cheese
   ("mummy's
   bandages")

1 cup broccoli florets
   ("ogre curls")

## TOOLS YOU NEED

• Liquid measuring
   cup (1 cup)
• Small serving bowl
• Wire whisk
• Measuring cups
• 7 small bowls

1 Measure out the salad dressing in the liquid measuring cup. Put it in the serving bowl. Add a few drops of green food color. Use the wire whisk to mix them together. If you want a darker green "slime," stir in a few more drops of food color.

2 Measure out the salad ingredients. Put them in 7 different bowls to create a salad bar. (Make labels so your friends know what's in the bowls.) Set the dressing out with the salad bar.

*1 Serving:* Calories 330; Total Fat 29g; Sodium 770mg; Total Carbohydrates 7g (Sugars 4g); Protein 12g • **Exchanges:** 1 Vegetable

**GET GROSS**
There are lots of other foods that can be used to creep out your guests. Green bell pepper strips can be "goblin fingers." Ham cubes could be labeled "finger tips." Frozen grapes can also double as "eyeballs." You may never look at food the same way again.

# Ghosts on Broomsticks

TIME IT TAKES: 1 hour 15 minutes • HOW MUCH IT MAKES: 14 ghost candies

## INGREDIENTS

1 chewy fruit snack in 3-foot roll (pick your favorite flavor)

14 pretzel sticks (2 to 3 inches long)

2/3 cup white vanilla chips

1 teaspoon miniature semisweet chocolate chips

## TOOLS YOU NEED

• Waxed or parchment paper
• Large cookie sheet
• Kitchen scissors
• Ruler
• Measuring cups
• Small saucepan (1 quart)
• Wooden spoon
• Measuring spoons

1 Tear off 1 sheet of waxed paper. Put it on the cookie sheet. Unwrap and unroll the fruit snack roll. Use the kitchen scissors to cut 1/2-inch-long fringe along 1 long side of the snack roll. Cut the fringed roll into 2-inch pieces. Count out 14 pretzel sticks.

2 To make each broomstick, wrap a piece of fringe around 1 end of a pretzel so the fringe part is to the outside. Use your fingers to press the fringe on the pretzel so it sticks. Put the broomsticks on the waxed paper-lined cookie sheet.

3 Measure out the white vanilla chips. Put them in the saucepan. Heat the chips over low heat, stirring a lot with the wooden spoon, until the chips are melted. Take the saucepan off the hot burner.

4 For each ghost, measure out a rounded 1/2 teaspoon of the melted chips and drop it crosswise onto the pretzel. Use your fingers to shape the melted chips to look like ghosts on broomsticks. (See the photo for how the shapes should look.)

5 Press 3 miniature chocolate chips onto each ghost for the eyes and nose. Let the ghosts sit on the kitchen counter for about 45 minutes or put them in the freezer for about 5 minutes, until the ghosts harden. Carefully peel the ghost candies off the waxed paper.

*1 Ghost Candy:* Calories 50; Total Fat 3g; Sodium 20mg; Total Carbohydrates 7g (Sugars 6g); Protein 0g • *Exchanges:* Free

## NUKE IT
You can melt the white vanilla chips in the microwave instead of on top of the stove. Put them in a small microwavable dish and microwave on High for 30 seconds. Stir until the chips are melted.

# Tidbits

# & Bites

## Bite-size finger foods and snacks

# Pizza Snacks

TIME IT TAKES: 45 minutes • HOW MUCH IT MAKES: 40 snacks

## INGREDIENTS

1 can (12 ounces)
   refrigerated flaky
   biscuits
3/4 cup pizza sauce
80 pepperoni slices
   (from two 3.5-ounce
   packages)
1 cup shredded
   mozzarella cheese
   (4 ounces)

## TOOLS YOU NEED

• Cooking spray
• 2 cookie sheets
• Measuring cups
• Measuring spoons
• Table knife
• Pot holders
• Pancake turner
• Wire cooling rack

1 Heat oven to 400°F. Spray the cookie sheet with cooking spray.

2 Remove the dough from the can. Separate it into 10 biscuits. Separate each biscuit into 4 layers and put each layer on the cookie sheets.

3 Measure out the pizza sauce. Use the knife to spread each biscuit layer with about 1 teaspoon of the pizza sauce. Put 2 pepperoni slices on each of the biscuit layers. Measure out the cheese. Put about 2 teaspoons of cheese on top of each biscuit layer.

4 Bake the pizza snacks for 7 to 9 minutes or until they look golden brown. Carefully take the cookie sheets out of the oven with the pot holders. Use the pancake turner to remove the pizza snacks from the cookie sheets and put them on the wire rack to cool.

*1 Snack: Calories 60; Total Fat 4g; Sodium 240mg; Total Carbohydrates 5g (Sugars 2g); Protein 2g • Exchanges: Free*

### PIZZA PARLOR
You can leave off the pepperoni if you don't like it and just make cheese pizzas. If that's the case, check out all the different kinds of cheeses there are at the grocery store and experiment to find your favorite.

# Mexi-Mix

**TIME IT TAKES: 20 minutes • HOW MUCH IT MAKES: 12 servings (1/2 cup each)**

## INGREDIENTS

3 cups bite-size baked cheese crackers

2 cups twisted butter-flavored pretzel sticks

1 cup salted peanuts

1 tablespoon vegetable oil

2 tablespoons taco seasoning mix (from a package)

## TOOLS YOU NEED

- Measuring cups
- Microwavable bowl (2 1/2 quart)
- Measuring spoons
- Wooden spoon
- Pot holders
- Waxed paper

**1** Measure out the crackers. Toss them into the bowl. Measure out the pretzel sticks. Toss them into the bowl. Measure out the peanuts. Toss them into the bowl, too.

**2** Measure out the oil. Drizzle it over the crackers, pretzels sticks and peanuts in the bowl. Stir with the wooden spoon so everything gets coated with oil. Measure out the taco seasoning mix. Sprinkle it over the mixture. Gently stir again with the wooden spoon so everything gets covered with the taco seasoning as much as possible.

**3** Microwave the mixture on High 2 minutes. Stir the mixture with the wooden spoon. Microwave on High another 2 minutes. Carefully take the bowl out of the microwave with the pot holders. Spoon the mixture onto a sheet of waxed paper. Let it cool for 5 minutes before eating.

*1/2 Cup: Calories 190; Total Fat 11g; Sodium 400mg; Total Carbohydrates 18g (Sugars 3g); Protein 6g • **Exchanges:** 1 Starch*

**SPICE IT UP**
You'll have some taco seasoning left over after making this mix. Instead of throwing it away, use it to sprinkle over popcorn to add some zing.

# Creamy Applesauce Dunk

TIME IT TAKES: 10 minutes • HOW MUCH IT MAKES: 2 servings (1/4 cup dip and 10 animal crackers each)

## INGREDIENTS

### DUNK
1/2 cup applesauce
2 tablespoons vanilla low-fat yogurt
1/8 teaspoon ground cinnamon

### DUNKERS
(CHOOSE YOUR FAVORITE)
Animal crackers
Chocolate graham crackers
Rainbow-colored vanilla wafers
Sweetened miniature shredded wheat cereal

## TOOLS YOU NEED
• Measuring cups
• Small bowl
• Rubber spatula
• Measuring spoons
• Spoon

1  Measure out the applesauce. Put it in the bowl. Scrape all of it out of the measuring cup with the rubber spatula.

2  Measure out the yogurt. Put it in the bowl. Measure out the cinnamon. Put it in the bowl, too. Mix everything together with the spoon.

3  Dip your favorite dunkers in the dip.

*1 Serving: Calories 170; Total Fat 4g; Sodium 115mg; Total Carbohydrates 33g (Sugars 21g); Protein 2g • Exchanges: 1 Starch, 1 Other Carbohydrate*

### ON THE RUN
This is a good snack to pack in a lunch. Put the dip in a plastic container with a tight lid and put the dunkers in a resealable food-storage plastic bag. Pop both in an insulated lunch bag and go!

# Cinnamon Twisties

**TIME IT TAKES:** 30 minutes • **HOW MUCH IT MAKES:** 6 servings (4 twisties each)

## INGREDIENTS

1 can (8 ounces) refrigerated crescent dinner rolls

1 tablespoon butter or margarine (from a stick)

2 teaspoons cinnamon-sugar blend

## TOOLS YOU NEED

- Cookie sheet
- Cooking spray
- Large cutting board (at least 13 x 8 inch)
- Ruler
- Table knife
- Custard cup
- Pastry brush
- Measuring spoons
- Pizza cutter
- Pot holders
- Pancake turner
- Wire cooling rack

**1** Heat the oven to 375°F.

**2** Lightly spray the cookie sheet with the cooking spray. Remove the dough from the can. Put on the cutting board. Unroll the dough into 1 large rectangle. Use your fingers to seal the perforations in the dough. (Perforations are tiny cuts in the dough that look like little lines.) Press out the dough to make a rectangle that is 12 inches long and 7 inches wide.

**3** Use the table knife to cut off 1 tablespoon from the stick of butter. (See the How-To Photo.) Put it in the custard cup. Put the rest of the butter back in the refrigerator. Microwave the butter on High 5 to 10 seconds, until it is melted. Use the pastry brush to brush the dough with the melted butter.

**4** Measure out the cinnamon-sugar blend. Sprinkle it evenly over the butter on the dough. Use the pizza cutter to cut the dough crosswise into 12 strips that are 7 inches long and 1 inch wide. Now cut the strips in half crosswise, so they are only 3 1/2 inches long. You should now have 24 strips. Twist each strip and put it on the cookie sheet.

**5** Bake the twisted strips for 8 to 10 minutes or until they look deep golden brown. Carefully take the cookie sheet out of the oven with the pot holders. Use the pancake turner to remove the cinnamon twisties from the cookie sheet and put them on the wire rack. Let them cool for about 5 minutes before you eat them, or let them cool completely.

*4 Twisties:* Calories 150; Total Fat 7g; Sodium 470mg; Total Carbohydrates 19g (Sugars 7g); Protein 3g • *Exchanges:* 1 Starch

> **GET DIPPY**
> These Cinnamon Twisties taste even better when you dip them in yogurt or pudding.

# Frosty Choco-Banana Snacks

TIME IT TAKES: 1 hour 30 minutes • HOW MUCH IT MAKES: 5 servings
(2 banana chunks each)

## INGREDIENTS

2 medium bananas

1 teaspoon
multicolored candy
sprinkles

1/3 cup semisweet
chocolate chips

1/3 cup milk chocolate
ready-to-spread
frosting

## TOOLS YOU NEED

• Waxed paper
• Large plate
• Table knife
• Cutting board
• 10 toothpicks
• Measuring spoons
• Custard cup
• Measuring cups
• Small microwavable
  bowl
• Spoon
• Rubber spatula

1  Put 1 piece of waxed paper on the plate. Peel the bananas. Use the table knife to cut each banana into 5 chunks on the cutting board.

2  Put the banana chunks, cut side down, on the waxed paper-lined plate. Stick a toothpick into each banana chunk. Put the plate in the freezer for about 20 minutes or until the banana chunks are hard.

3  While the banana chunks are freezing, measure out the candy sprinkles. Put them in the custard cup. Set them aside for later. Measure out the chocolate chips. Toss them into the bowl. Microwave the chips on High 60 to 90 seconds, until they are melted. Stir the chocolate chips with the spoon until they are smooth.

4  Measure out the frosting. Use the rubber spatula to scrape all of it out of the measuring cup and into the bowl with the melted chips. Mix it all up with the spoon. Microwave the mixture on High 15 to 20 seconds, until the mixture looks like a dip.

5  Remove the banana chunks from the freezer. Dip each banana chunk into the melted chocolate mixture. Spoon some chocolate onto the sides of each chunk. Sprinkle the banana chunks with the candy sprinkles from the cup you set aside earlier. When you are finished putting the sprinkles on the banana chunks, put them back on the waxed paper-lined plate.

6  Put the dipped banana chunks in the freezer for 1 hour or until the chocolate and bananas are hard. Eat the banana chunks right out of the freezer.

*2 Banana Chunks: Calories 190; Total Fat 8g; Sodium 0mg; Total Carbohydrates 30g (Sugars 23g); Protein 1g • Exchanges: 1 Fruit, 1 Other Carbohydrate*

## DOUBLE DIPPING
If the chocolate chip and frosting mixture starts to get hard, microwave it on High 5 to 10 seconds, until it gets soft again.

# Sparkly Popcorn

TIME IT TAKES: 15 minutes  •  HOW MUCH IT MAKES: 8 servings (1 cup each)

## INGREDIENTS

1 snack-size bag
  (1.75 ounces)
  microwave popcorn
2 cups Trix cereal
1 tablespoon edible
  glitter

## TOOLS YOU NEED

• Large bowl
• Measuring cups
• Wooden spoon
• Measuring spoons

**1**  Microwave the bag of popcorn as directed on the bag. Be careful when you open the bag of popcorn. Hot steam will come out. You should wind up with about 6 cups of popped popcorn. Toss the popped popcorn into the bowl.

**2**  Measure out the cereal. Toss it into the bowl. Gently mix the popcorn and cereal together with the wooden spoon.

**3**  Measure out the edible glitter. Sprinkle it over the top of the popcorn mixture.

*1 Cup:* Calories 70; Total Fat 2 1/2g; Sodium 100mg; Total Carbohydrates 11g (Sugars 5g); Protein 0g • **Exchanges:** Free

**GLITTER FOR YOUR MOUTH**
In search of sparkle? You can find it at craft stores in the cake decorating department or baking specialty stores. If you still have trouble tracking it down, just use your favorite colored sugar instead.

# Lemony Fruit Dip

**TIME IT TAKES:** 1 hour 40 minutes • **HOW MUCH IT MAKES:** 4 servings
(1/3 cup dip and 1/2 apple each)

## INGREDIENTS

1/4 cup pineapple
 cream cheese spread
1 container (8 ounces)
 lemon low-fat yogurt
1/4 cup dried fruit and
 raisin mixture
2 large apples

## TOOLS YOU NEED

• Measuring cups
• Small bowl
• Rubber spatula
• Wooden spoon
• Plastic wrap
• Cutting board
• Sharp knife
• Spoon
• 4 custard cups

1  Measure out the cream cheese spread. Put it in the bowl. Scrape all of it out of the measuring cup with the rubber spatula. Mix the cream cheese spread with the rubber spatula. Add the yogurt to the bowl. Scrape all of it out of the container with the rubber spatula. Mix on low speed until everything is mixed together.

2  Measure out the fruit and raisin mixture. Put it in the bowl. Stir everything together with the wooden spoon.

3  Cover the bowl with plastic wrap. Put it in the refrigerator for at least 1 1/2 hours or overnight.

4  When you are ready to eat the dip, wash the apples. Put them on the cutting board. Use the sharp knife to cut each apple in half, from top to bottom. Cut each half in half again, so now you have 4 pieces from each apple. Cut out the seeds and cut each apple piece into slices.

5  Spoon about the same amount of the dip into each of the custard cups. Serve the dip with the apple slices.

*1 Serving:* Calories 190; Total Fat 6g; Sodium 80mg; Total Carbohydrates 33g (Sugars 28g); Protein 4g • *Exchanges:* 1 Fat

### OTHER DUNKERS
Can you think of some other foods to dip into this fruity dip? How about orange slices or pieces of pear? Try sticking grapes on a toothpick and dunking them into the dip.

# Crackerpillars

TIME IT TAKES: 35 minutes • HOW MUCH IT MAKES: 4 caterpillars

## INGREDIENTS

28 miniature buttery round peanut butter-filled cracker sandwiches

2 tablespoons creamy peanut butter

8 miniature semisweet chocolate chips

8 pieces black string licorice (each 1 inch long)

32 miniature candy-coated chocolate baking bits

Red decorating gel · (from a tube)

## TOOLS YOU NEED

• Measuring spoons
• Custard cup
• Rubber spatula
• Table knife
• Serving plate

1  Count out 28 cracker sandwiches. Divide them into piles of 7 cracker sandwiches each. You should have 4 piles. Each pile will make 1 crackerpillar.

2  Measure out the peanut butter. Put it in the custard cup. Scrape all of it out of the measuring spoon with the rubber spatula.

3  To make 1 crackerpillar, use the table knife to spread a tiny bit of peanut butter on 6 of the cracker sandwiches in the pile. Stack them on top of each other so that the last cracker sandwich has peanut butter on top. Put the last cracker sandwich from the pile, the one that doesn't have any peanut butter on it, on the very top.

4  Lay the stack on its side. Move the cracker sandwiches just a little so that the stack makes an "S" shape like a crackerpillar. Put the crackerpillar on the plate. Make the other 3 crackerpillars the same way.

5  To make the eyes, attach 2 miniature chocolate chips with a tiny dab of peanut butter on 1 end of each crackerpillar. Stick 2 pieces of licorice between the first 2 cracker sandwiches to make the crackerpillar's antennae. Attach 4 baking bits with peanut butter along each side of each crackerpillar to make the legs. Squeeze the decorating gel to paint on the mouths.

*1 Crackerpillar:* Calories 140; Total Fat 9g; Sodium 170mg; Total Carbohydrates 13g (Sugars 4g); Protein 3g • *Exchanges:* 1 Starch

### CRACKERPILLAR PARK
Just for fun, create a "playground" on the serving plate for your crackerpillars. Smash up some chocolate wafer cookies to make "dirt," and color some coconut green for "grass."

# Baked Apples with Granola

TIME IT TAKES: 15 minutes • HOW MUCH IT MAKES: 2 servings

## INGREDIENTS

1 large crisp apple

1 tablespoon raisins or sweetened dried cranberries

1 tablespoon brown sugar

2 teaspoons butter or margarine (from a stick)

1/2 cup granola

## TOOLS YOU NEED

• Sharp knife
• Cutting board
• Spoon
• 2 small microwavable bowls
• Measuring spoons
• Table knife
• Custard cup
• Microwavable plastic wrap
• Measuring cups

**1** Use the sharp knife to cut the apple in half from top to bottom on the cutting board. Use the spoon to scoop out the seeds and core of the apple. Throw the seeds and core away. Put an apple half in each bowl.

**2** Measure out the raisins. Sprinkle them equally on each of the apple halves. Measure out the brown sugar. Sprinkle it equally over the two apple halves. Use the table knife to cut off 2 teaspoons from the stick of butter. Put it in the custard cup. Put the rest of the butter back in the refrigerator. Use the table knife to cut the butter in the custard cup in half (each half is 1 teaspoon). Put 1 teaspoon of butter on top of each apple half. Cover each bowl with plastic wrap. Leave a little of the bowl uncovered so the steam can escape.

**3** Microwave each apple half on High for 2 1/2 to 3 minutes or until the apple is kind of soft when you touch it. Be careful when you take off the plastic wrap because hot air will come out. Measure out the granola. Sprinkle the granola over each apple half.

*1 Serving: Calories 230; Total Fat 5g; Sodium 90mg; Total Carbohydrates 46g (Sugars 31g); Protein 2g • Exchanges: 1 Fat*

### APPLE PICKING
Some apples are better to use in cooking than others. Some good kinds of apples to use in this recipe are Braeburn, Gala or Fuji. They won't get as mushy as other kinds (yuck!).

# Peanutty Rice Cake Rounds

TIME IT TAKES: 20 minutes • HOW MUCH IT MAKES: 6 servings (2 rounds each)

## INGREDIENTS

1/4 cup creamy or
  crunchy peanut
  butter
1 teaspoon honey
3 fresh whole
  strawberries
24 miniature rice
  cakes

## TOOLS YOU NEED

• Measuring cups
• Small bowl
• Rubber spatula
• Measuring spoons
• Wooden spoon
• Colander
• Paper towels
• Sharp knife
• Cutting board
• Table knife

**1** Measure out the peanut butter. Put it in the bowl. Scrape all of it out of the measuring cup with the rubber spatula.

**2** Measure out the honey. Put it in the bowl. Mix them up with the wooden spoon until the mixture is smooth.

**3** Put the colander in the sink. Put the strawberries in the colander. Rinse them with cold water. Put the washed strawberries on the paper towels and pat them dry. Use the sharp knife to remove the stems from the strawberries on the cutting board. (See the How-To Photo.) Cut each strawberry sideways into 4 round slices.

**4** Use the table knife to spread some peanut butter mixture on each rice cake. Put 1 slice of strawberry on top of 12 of the rice cakes. Take the other 12 rice cakes and stack them, peanut butter side down, on top of the strawberries.

*2 Rounds:* Calories 100; Total Fat 6g; Sodium 75mg; Total Carbohydrates 10g (Sugars 2g); Protein 3g • *Exchanges:* Free

## ALL SHOOK UP
If you're like Elvis and you enjoy peanut butter and bananas together, use slices of bananas instead of strawberry slices in these rad rice cake rounds.

# Crunchy Biscuit Bites

TIME IT TAKES: 20 minutes • HOW MUCH IT MAKES: 32 biscuit bites

## INGREDIENTS

2 tablespoons sugar

1/2 teaspoon ground cinnamon

1 can (10.2 ounces) large refrigerated buttermilk homestyle biscuits

2 tablespoons butter or margarine (from a stick)

3/4 cup finely crushed Cinnamon Toast Crunch® cereal

## TOOLS YOU NEED

• Cookie sheet
• Cooking spray
• Measuring spoons
• Large bowl
• Spoon
• Kitchen scissors
• Wooden spoon
• Table knife
• Custard cup
• Resealable food-storage plastic bag (quart size)
• Rolling pin
• Pot holders
• Pancake turner

1  Heat the oven to 400°F. Spray the cookie sheet with cooking spray.

2  Measure out the sugar. Put it in the bowl. Measure out the cinnamon. Put it in the bowl, too. Mix it up with the spoon.

3  Remove the dough from the can. Separate it into 5 biscuits. Use the kitchen scissors to cut each biscuit into 6 equal wedges. Put the biscuit wedges in the bowl with the sugar and cinnamon. Stir the dough wedges around the bowl with the wooden spoon.

4  Use the table knife to cut off 2 tablespoons from the stick of butter. Put it in the custard cup. Put the rest of the butter back in the refrigerator. Microwave the butter on High 20 to 30 seconds, until it is melted.

5  Use the spoon to drizzle the butter over the dough wedges in the bowl. Stir the dough wedges around in the bowl with the wooden spoon so they get covered in butter as much as possible.

6  Put some cereal in the plastic bag. Seal the bag, trying to get as much of the air out as you can. Use the rolling pin to crush the cereal. Keep adding cereal until you can measure out 3/4 cup. Add the crushed cereal to the dough wedges in the bowl. Gently stir with the wooden spoon so the dough wedges get covered with cereal as much as possible.

7  Place the biscuit wedges in rows on the cookie sheet. Make sure their sides are not touching.

8  Bake the dough wedges for 13 minutes or until they look golden brown. Carefully take the cookie sheet out of the oven with the pot holders. Use the pancake turner to remove the biscuit bites from the cookie sheet. Serve them warm.

*4 Biscuit Bites: Calories 70; Total Fat 4g; Sodium 95mg; Total Carbohydrates 9g (Sugars 4g); Protein 0g • Exchanges: Free*

## MORNING MUNCHIES

Even though these cinnamon, sugar and cereal biscuit bites are in the snack chapter, you could also eat them in the morning for breakfast.

# Alphabet Dunkers

TIME IT TAKES: 30 minutes • HOW MUCH IT MAKES: 6 servings (2 letters and 3 tablespoons sauce each)

## INGREDIENTS

1 can (11 ounce) refrigerated breadsticks

1 cup pizza sauce

## TOOLS YOU NEED

• Cookie sheet
• Measuring cups
• Small saucepan
• Small serving dish
• Pot holders
• Pancake turner

1  Heat the oven to 375ºF.

2  Remove the dough from the can. Unroll the dough and separate it at the perforations to form 12 strips. (Perforations are tiny cuts in the dough that look like little lines.) Shape the strips of dough on the cookie sheet into any letters you want. (You do not need to grease the cookie sheet.)

3  Bake the dough letters for 13 to 15 minutes or until they look golden brown.

4  While the dough letters are baking, measure out the pizza sauce. Put it in the small saucepan. Heat the pizza sauce over medium heat until it is hot all the way through. Pour the sauce into the dish.

5  Carefully take the cookie sheet out of the oven with the pot holders. Use the pancake turner to remove the letters from the cookie sheet. Serve the warm letters with the warm pizza sauce for dipping.

*1 Serving: Calories 170; Total Fat 4g; Sodium 550mg; Total Carbohydrates 28g (Sugars 4g); Protein 5g • Exchanges: 2 Starch*

### FLAVOR BOOST
To give these dough letters cheesy, sprinkle a little Parmesan cheese over the top of the dough before you bake them.

# Slumber

# Party

Forget sleep,
it's time to eat!

# Chicken in a Sleeping Bag

**TIME IT TAKES: 1 hour 40 minutes • HOW MUCH IT MAKES: 8 sandwiches**

## INGREDIENTS

16 frozen breaded chicken breast tenders

2 cans (8 ounces each) refrigerated crescent dinner rolls

8 slices (1 ounce each) cooked ham

8 slices (3/4 ounce each) Swiss process cheese food

Ketchup and mustard in squirt bottles, if desired

## TOOLS YOU NEED

• Large plate
• Plastic wrap
• Ruler
• Cookie sheet
• Fork
• Pot holders
• Pancake turner
• 8 serving plates

**1** Count out 16 frozen chicken breast tenders. Put them on the plate. Cover the plate with plastic wrap. Put the plate in the refrigerator and let the chicken tenders thaw for 1 hour.

**2** Heat the oven to 375ºF.

**3** Remove the dough from both cans. Unroll each roll. Separate both rolls of dough so you have 8 rectangles. Each rectangle should be about 7 1/2 inches long and 4 inches wide. Press the perforations in each rectangle together with your fingers. (Perforations are tiny cuts in the dough that look like little lines.)

**4** For each sandwich, put 1 dough rectangle on the cookie sheet. (You do not need to grease the cookie sheet.) Top the rectangle with 1 slice of ham. Put 1 slice of cheese at 1 end of the ham slice, where the heads will go. Put 2 chicken tenders on top of the cheese. Fold the dough over the chicken tenders to cover them up a little more than halfway. Press the sides of the dough with the fork to seal the edges. Do the same thing to make all the other sandwiches.

**5** Bake the sandwiches for 15 to 17 minutes or until they look golden brown and the chicken is hot. Carefully take the cookie sheet out of the oven with the pot holders. Use the pancake turner to remove the sandwiches from the cookie sheet and put them on the plates.

**6** Squirt ketchup and mustard on the chicken tenders to make faces.

*1 Sandwich: Calories 430; Total Fat 23g; Sodium 1,650mg; Total Carbohydrates 33g (Sugars 9g); Protein 23g • Exchanges: 2 Starch, 2 1/2 Lean Meat, 3 Fat*

### HURRY IT UP

If you can't wait 1 hour for the chicken tenders to thaw in the refrigerator, microwave them instead. Put them on a large microwavable plate and microwave on Low 2 to 4 minutes, until thawed. Take the plate of chicken out of the microwave.

# Jiggly Fruit Salad

TIME IT TAKES: 2 hours 25 minutes • HOW MUCH IT MAKES: 10 squares

## INGREDIENTS

1 can (11 ounces) mandarin orange segments

1 can (20 ounces) pineapple tidbits in juice

2 envelopes unflavored gelatin

3 cups berry-flavored carrot and fruit juice blend

1 package (10 ounces) frozen sliced strawberries in syrup

2 medium bananas

## TOOLS YOU NEED

• Can opener
• Colander
• Glass baking dish (13 x 9 inch or 3 quart)
• Liquid measuring cup (4 cup)
• Medium saucepan (2 quart)
• Wooden spoon
• Table knife
• Cutting board
• Sharp knife

1 Use the can opener to open the can of mandarin orange segments and the can of pineapple tidbits. Put the colander in the baking dish. Pour the orange segments and pineapple tidbits into the colander so all the liquid drains into the dish. Take the colander of fruit out of the baking dish and set it aside. You'll use it later.

2 Sprinkle the gelatin on top of the liquid in the baking dish. Let the gelatin stand for about 5 minutes so it softens.

3 While the gelatin is softening, measure out the berry-flavored juice blend in the liquid measuring cup. Pour it into the saucepan. Heat the juice over medium-high heat until it bubbles.

4 Carefully pour the bubbling juice over the softened gelatin in the baking dish. Use the wooden spoon to stir the mixture until you can't see the little gelatin specks anymore. Add the strawberries to the gelatin mixture. Stir it with the wooden spoon until it gets kind of thick. Break up the strawberries if they are stuck together.

5 Add the orange segments and pineapple tidbits you set aside earlier to the gelatin mixture. Peel the bananas. Use the table knife to cut the bananas into slices on the cutting board. Toss the banana slices into the mixture, too.

6 Stir everything together until it's all mixed up. Put the dish in the refrigerator for at least 2 hours or until the fruit salad looks solid.

7 To serve the salad, use the sharp knife to cut it into 2 rows by 5 rows. You should now have 10 squares.

*1 Square: Calories 140; Total Fat 0g; Sodium 15mg; Total Carbohydrates 34g (Sugars 28g); Protein 3g • Exchanges: 1 Starch, 1 Fruit*

**IS IT MAGIC?**
Gelatin doesn't smell or taste. It is used to thicken foods. When you dissolve gelatin in hot water and let it cool, like you do in this fruit salad, it turns into a jelly. Cool, huh?

# Truth-or-Dare Chocolate-Strawberry Cupcakes

**TIME IT TAKES: 50 minutes • HOW MUCH IT MAKES: 8 cupcakes**

## INGREDIENTS

1 tub (8 ounces) strawberry cream cheese spread

1/2 cup powdered sugar

1 tablespoon milk

1 cup frozen (thawed) whipped topping

8 unfrosted chocolate cupcakes (from the store or made with a cake mix)

4 fresh whole strawberries

## TOOLS YOU NEED

- Kitchen scissors
- Sheets of paper (8 1/2 x 11 inches each)
- Pen, pencil or another writing utensil
- Ruler
- Foil
- Colorful curly ribbon
- Large bowl
- Rubber spatula
- Spoon
- Measuring cups
- Measuring spoons
- Resealable freezer plastic bag (1 quart)
- Colander
- Paper towels
- Sharp knife
- Cutting board

**1** Use the kitchen scissors to cut the 2 sheets of paper into 8 squares that are 3 inches long and 3 inches wide. Write a truth-or-dare message on each square of paper. Roll up each paper square into a tiny tube.

**2** Tear off 1 piece of foil about 12 inches long and 5 inches wide. Use the scissors to cut the foil into 8 strips that are 2 inches wide and 5 inches long. Wrap 1 foil strip around each scroll to cover it up. Squeeze 1 end of each foil-wrapped scroll to form a point. Use a few strands of ribbon to tie the other end of the foil closed. Set the foil-wrapped scrolls aside. You'll use them later.

**3** Put the cream cheese spread in the bowl. Scrape all of it out of the tub with the rubber spatula. Stir the cream cheese spread with the spoon until it gets soft. Measure out the powdered sugar and milk. Put them in the bowl. Stir everything in the bowl until the mixture looks smooth.

**4** Measure out the whipped topping. Fold the whipped topping into the cream cheese mixture. (To learn how to fold, see page 8.)

**5** Spoon the fluffy mixture into the plastic bag. Seal the bag, trying to get as much of the air out as you can. Use the scissors to cut a 1/2-inch hole in the bottom corner of the bag. Squeeze the bag in a circular motion to make the frosting come out in spiral shapes on top of the cupcakes.

**6** Put the colander in the sink. Put the strawberries in the colander. Rinse them with cold water. Put the washed strawberries on paper towels. Pat them dry. Use the sharp knife to remove the stems from the strawberries on the cutting board. Cut each strawberry in half, from top to bottom, with the knife. Press 1 strawberry half, with the rounded side up, on top of each cupcake.

**7** Push the pointed end of 1 truth-or-dare scroll partway into the top of each cupcake.

*1 Cupcake: Calories 230; Total Fat 15g; Sodium 210mg; Total Carbohydrates 21g (Sugars 16g); Protein 3g • Exchanges: 1/2 Starch, 1 Other Carbohydrate, 3 Fat*

**SILLY SCROLLS**
How many truth-or-dares can you think of? Here are two ideas to get you started: Truth—If you could pick any boy or girl in your school, who would you pick to be your boyfriend or girlfriend? Dare—Eat a dill pickle dipped in peanut butter.

# Worth

# the Wait

## Save room for these delicious desserts

# Pretty Posy Cookies

TIME IT TAKES: 1 hour • HOW MUCH IT MAKES: 20 cookies

## INGREDIENTS

20 pastel melty mint drop candies (about 1 inch each)

4 colored sugars (about 2 tablespoons of each)

1 package (18 ounces) refrigerated ready-to-bake sugar cookie dough (20 cookies)

## TOOLS YOU NEED

- Parchment paper or foil
- 2 or 3 cookie sheets
- Measuring spoons
- 4 custard cups
- Cutting board
- Table knife
- Pot holders
- Pancake turner
- Wire cooling racks

**1** Heat the oven to 350ºF.

**2** Tear off 2 or 3 pieces of parchment paper. Put 1 piece on each cookie sheet. Count out 20 mint candies. Set them aside. You'll use them later. Measure out 2 tablespoons of each color of sugar. Put each of the colored sugars in a different custard cup.

**3** Take the cookie dough chunks out of the package. For each posy cookie, put 1 unbaked cookie dough round on the cutting board. Use the table knife to cut it into 4 wedges. Roll each wedge of cookie dough in a different color of sugar to cover it all over. Arrange the wedges on 1 of the paper-lined cookie sheets in a flower shape. The flowers should not touch each other and should be about 1 inch apart. They will puff up and get bigger when they bake.

**4** Bake the cookies for 12 to 16 minutes or until the edges look golden brown. Carefully take the cookie sheets out of the oven with the pot holders. Press 1 mint candy, pointy side down, into the middle of each cookie. Use the pancake turner to remove the cookies from the cookie sheets and put them on the wire racks to cool.

*1 Cookie: Calories 130; Total Fat 3 1/2g; Sodium 85mg; Total Carbohydrates 24g (Sugars 17g); Protein 1g • Exchanges: 1/2 Starch, 1 Other Carbohydrate, 1/2 Fat*

### RAINBOW FLOWERS
You don't have to limit yourself to only 4 colors of petals on your cookies. If you have lots of different colors of sugar, use them all so your flowers are all kinds of pretty colors.

# Sugar Cookie Shortcake

TIME IT TAKES: 2 hours 20 minutes • HOW MUCH IT MAKES: 10 servings

## INGREDIENTS

1 roll (18 ounces) refrigerated sugar cookie dough

2 tablespoons sugar

1 quart fresh whole strawberries (4 cups)

1 box (3.4 ounces) instant vanilla pudding and pie filling mix

1 cup cold milk

1 1/2 cups frozen (thawed) whipped topping

## TOOLS YOU NEED

• Foil
• 2 round pans (9 inch each)
• Cutting board
• Table knife
• Measuring spoons
• Pot holders
• Wire cooling racks
• Colander
• Paper towels
• Sharp knife
• Small bowl
• Liquid measuring cup (1 cup)

*(continued on next page)*

**1** Heat the oven to 350ºF.

**2** Tear off 2 pieces of foil about 12 inches long and 12 inches wide. Turn the 2 pans upside down. Cover the upside-down pans with foil. Press the foil down around the side of each pan. Take the foil off the pans. Turn the pans right side up. Now put the foil inside each pan, pushing it carefully into the bottom so the inside of each pan is completely covered with foil. Fold the top of the foil down over the edge of each pan.

**3** Remove the cookie dough from the wrapper. Put the dough on the cutting board. Use the table knife to cut the roll of cookie dough in half the long way. You should wind up with 2 long skinny pieces of dough. Put 1 piece of dough in each of the foil-lined pans. Use your fingers to press out the dough in each pan so it covers the bottom. (If your fingers get sticky, dip them in a little flour.)

**4** Measure out 1 tablespoon sugar. Sprinkle it over 1 cookie layer. Do the same thing with the other tablespoon of sugar for the other cookie layer.

**5** Bake the cookie layers for 20 minutes or until they look light golden brown. Carefully take the pans out of the oven with the pot holders and put them on the wire racks. Let the cookie layers cool for 10 minutes.

**6** After the 10 minutes, carefully lift the cookie layers out of the pans by pulling up on the foil. Put the cookie layers on the wire racks. Let them cool for another 20 minutes.

**7** While the cookie layers are cooling, put the colander in the sink. Put the strawberries in the colander. Rinse them with cold water. Put the washed strawberries on the paper towels and pat them dry. Use the sharp knife to remove the stems from the strawberries on the cutting board. Cut each strawberry sideways into slices.

**8** Put the pudding mix in the bowl. Measure out the milk in the liquid measuring cup. Pour it into the bowl. Beat the pudding mix and the milk together with the wire whisk for about 2 minutes, until the mixture gets thick.

**9** Measure out the whipped topping. Fold the whipped topping into the milk and pudding mixture with the rubber spatula. (To learn how to fold, see page 8.) After you're done folding the whipped topping into the pudding, measure out 1/2 cup of it. Set it aside. You'll use it later.

*(continued from previous page)*

- Wire whisk
- Measuring cups
- Large serving plate (10 inch)
- Rubber spatula
- Spoon
- Long sharp knife

**LOOKING PRETTY**
If you want your shortcake to look extra nice, carefully arrange 10 fresh whole strawberries on the top.

**10** Remove the foil from the cookie layers. Put 1 cookie layer on the plate. Use the table knife to spread half of the pudding mixture on the cookie layer. Then put half of the strawberry slices on top of the pudding layer. Put the other cookie layer on top of the strawberries, like you're making a sandwich. Then top that cookie layer with the rest of the pudding mixture and the sliced strawberries that are left.

**11** Take the 1/2 cup of the pudding mixture you set aside earlier and spoon it onto the center of the shortcake. Refrigerate the shortcake at least 1 hour before serving. To serve it, use the long sharp knife to cut the shortcake into wedges.

*1 Serving: Calories 310; Total Fat 10g; Sodium 330mg; Total Carbohydrates 53g (Sugars 37g); Protein 3g • Exchanges: 1 Starch, 1/2 Fruit, 2 Other Carbohydrates, 2 Fat*

# S'mores Nachos

TIME IT TAKES: 10 minutes • HOW MUCH IT MAKES: 4 servings

## INGREDIENTS

8 graham cracker
  rectangles
3/4 cup milk chocolate
  chips
1 1/2 cups miniature
  marshmallows

## TOOLS YOU NEED

• Measuring cups
• Pie pan (9 inch)
• Pot holders

**1** Count out 8 graham crackers. Measure out the chocolate chips and the miniature marshmallows.

**2** Break each graham cracker into 4 pieces. Put the pieces in the pan. (Don't use a glass pan because it could break under the broiler.) Sprinkle the chocolate chips and the marshmallows over the graham crackers.

**3** Put the pan under the broiler about 6 inches from the heat. Broil for about 30 to 60 seconds, until the marshmallows get puffy and look light brown. Watch carefully so the s'mores don't burn. Carefully take the pie pan out from under the broiler with the pot holders. Don't let the pot holders touch the broiler or they might catch on fire.

*1 Serving:* Calories 340; Total Fat 12g; Sodium 190mg; Total Carbohydrates 55g
(Sugars 40g); Protein 4g • *Exchanges:* 1 Starch, 2 1/2 Other Carbohydrates, 2 Fat

**DID YOU KNOW?**
Know where s'mores got their name? They taste so good that when you eat them you always want "some more." S'mores are usually made outside over a campfire, but this indoor version can be made no matter what it's like outside.

# Peanut Butter Fudge-Topped Chippers

TIME IT TAKES: 45 minutes • HOW MUCH IT MAKES: 20 cookies

## INGREDIENTS

1/2 cup peanut butter chips

1/2 cup chocolate whipped ready-to-spread frosting

1 package (18 ounces) refrigerated ready-to-bake chocolate chip cookie dough (20 cookies)

## TOOLS YOU NEED

• Measuring cups
• Small saucepan (1 quart)
• Wooden spoon
• Rubber spatula
• Large cookie sheet
• Pot holders
• Pancake turner

**1** Heat the oven to 350°F.

**2** Measure out the peanut butter chips. Toss them into the saucepan. Heat the chips over low heat, stirring a lot with the wooden spoon, until they are melted. Remove the saucepan from the hot burner.

**3** Measure out the frosting. Use the rubber spatula to scrape all of it out of the measuring cup and into the saucepan. Stir the frosting and melted chips together with the wooden spoon. Cool the peanut butter mixture in the saucepan about 10 minutes so you can make it into shapes.

**4** Take the cookie dough chunks out of the package and put them on the cookie sheet. The dough rounds should not touch each other and should be 2 inches apart. (You do not need to grease the cookie sheet.) Bake the cookies for 10 to 14 minutes or until they look golden brown.

**5** While the cookies are baking, use your hands to shape the peanut butter mixture into 20 balls, each about 1 inch around.

**6** Carefully take the cookie sheet out of the oven with the pot holders. Right away, press 1 peanut butter ball into the center of each hot cookie. Let the cookies cool 2 minutes on the sheet. Then use the pancake turner to remove them from the cookie sheet.

*1 Cookie: Calories 180; Total Fat 8g; Sodium 110mg; Total Carbohydrates 23g (Sugars 14g); Protein 3g • Exchanges: 1 Starch, 1/2 Other Carbohydrate, 1 1/2 Fat*

### CHIPPERS, TAKE TWO
If you want your cookies to be extra chocolatey, use 1/2 cup chocolate chips instead of the peanut butter chips.

# Toaster Apple Sundaes

TIME IT TAKES: 15 minutes • HOW MUCH IT MAKES: 4 sundaes

## INGREDIENTS

4 toaster strudel
  frozen brown sugar
  cinnamon pastries
1 cup apple pie filling
2 cups vanilla ice
  cream

## TOOLS YOU NEED

• Toaster or toaster
  oven
• Can opener
• Measuring cup
• Small microwavable
  bowl
• Pot holders
• 4 serving plates
• Spoon
• Ice cream scoop
• Scissors

**1** Toast the pastries like the directions on the package say.

**2** While the pastries are in the toaster, open the can of apple pie filling with the can opener. Measure out the apple pie filling. Pour the apple pie filling into the bowl. Microwave the bowl on high for 1 minute or until the pie filling is hot.

**3** Carefully remove the pastries from the toaster with the pot holders. Put each of the pastries on a serving plate. Spoon some hot apple pie filling on each of the pastries. Use the ice cream scoop to put one scoop of ice cream on top of each pastry.

**4** Cut off a corner of the icing packet from the pastries package with the scissors. Drizzle the icing over each pastry.

*1 Sundae: Calories 410; Total Fat 15g; Sodium 240mg; Total Carbohydrates 66g (Sugars 41g); Protein 5g • Exchanges: 1 Starch, 3 1/2 Other Carbohydrates, 3 Fat*

### SWEET TOUCH
If you like sweet things, try drizzling a little caramel sauce over the top of these melt-in-your-mouth pastries.

# Thumbprint Heart Sugar Cookies

**TIME IT TAKES:** 1 hour 30 minutes • **HOW MUCH IT MAKES:** 32 cookies

## INGREDIENTS

1 roll (18 ounces)
  refrigerated sugar
  cookie dough
1 egg
10 drops red food
  color
1/4 cup sugar
Red decorating icing
  (from a tube)

## TOOLS YOU NEED

• Egg separator
• Custard cup
• Fork
• Cutting board
• Sharp knife
• Cookie sheets
• Measuring cups
• Pot holders
• Pancake turner
• Wire cooling racks

**1** Put the roll of cookie dough (still in the package) in the freezer and let it freeze for 30 minutes.

**2** Heat the oven to 350°F.

**3** Separate the egg using an egg separator. (See the How-To Photo.) Put the egg yolk in the custard cup. Use the white part of the egg to make scrambled eggs later, if you want.

**4** Beat the egg yolk with the fork. Add 10 drops of red food color to the beaten yolk. Mix it all up with the fork until it turns a nice red color.

**5** Take the cookie dough out of the freezer. Remove the dough from the wrapper. Put the dough on the cutting board. Use the sharp knife to cut the dough into 1/4-inch-thick slices. Put the slices of dough on the cookie sheets. (You do not need to grease the cookie sheets.) The slices of dough should not touch each other and should be about 2 inches apart.

**6** Dip your thumb or your pointer finger into the egg mixture so that it turns red. Press your red finger onto each cookie at an angle twice to make a heart shape. Measure out the sugar. Sprinkle a little sugar on each cookie.

**7** Bake the cookies for 7 to 11 minutes or until the edges look light golden brown. Carefully take the cookie sheet out of the oven with the pot holders. Let them cool 1 minute. Then use the pancake turner to remove the cookies from the cookie sheet and put them on the wire racks. Let the cookies cool 5 minutes or until they aren't warm when you touch them.

**8** Squeeze the icing to write names or messages on the cooled cookies.

**1 Cookie:** *Calories 110; Total Fat 3 1/2g; Sodium 55mg; Total Carbohydrates 19g (Sugars 15g); Protein 0g •* **Exchanges:** *1 Starch, 1/2 Fat*

# Ice Cream Tacos

**TIME IT TAKES:** 1 hour • **HOW MUCH IT MAKES:** 8 tacos

## INGREDIENTS

8 mini taco shells

1/3 cup milk chocolate chips

1 pint vanilla ice cream (2 cups)

2 tablespoons chopped peanuts

## TOOLS YOU NEED

- Loaf pan (9 x 5 inch)
- Foil
- Pot holders
- Measuring cups
- Measuring spoons
- Small microwavable dish
- Spoon

**1** Heat the oven to 350ºF.

**2** Stand the taco shells up in the loaf pan. If you need to, crumple up pieces of foil into balls. Stick them in the pan to prop up the taco shells.

**3** Heat the taco shells for 5 minutes or until they are crisp and look light golden brown. Carefully take the loaf pan out of the oven with the pot holders. Let the taco shells cool in the pan for 10 minutes or until they aren't warm when you touch them.

**4** Leave the taco shells in the pan. Measure out the chocolate chips. Spoon 1 teaspoon into the bottom of each taco shell. Set aside the chocolate chips. You'll use them later. Measure out 1/4 cup of the ice cream. Put it in 1 taco shell. Fill each of the other taco shells with 1/4 cup ice cream, too. Freeze the tacos in the pan for 15 minutes.

**5** While the tacos are freezing, put the chocolate chips you set aside earlier into the dish. Microwave the chips on High 1 to 2 minutes, until the chocolate is smooth when you stir it with the spoon. Measure out the chopped peanuts.

**6** Remove the tacos from the freezer. Use the spoon to drizzle the melted chocolate over the top of each taco. Right away, sprinkle the chopped peanuts over the chocolate. Freeze the tacos again for at least 10 minutes so the chocolate gets hard before you eat them.

*1 Taco: Calories 140; Total Fat 8g; Sodium 60mg; Total Carbohydrates 15g (Sugars 10g); Protein 3g • Exchanges: 1 Starch, 1 1/2 Fat*

**SUMMERTIME SNACK**
Store a few of these Ice Cream Tacos in the freezer for an icy cool, crunchy bite on a hot summer day.

# Night Crawler Cupcakes

TIME IT TAKES: 1 hour 20 minutes • HOW MUCH IT MAKES: 24 cupcakes

## INGREDIENTS

1 1/4 cups water

1/3 cup vegetable oil

3 eggs

1 box (18.25 ounces) yellow cake mix with pudding

3/4 cup chocolate ready-to-spread frosting

24 gummy worm candies

## TOOLS YOU NEED

• 24 paper baking cups
• 2 medium muffin pans (12 cups in each)
• Cooking spray
• Liquid measuring cup (1 cup each)
• Custard cup
• Small bowl
• Pot holders
• Wire cooling racks
• Wooden spoon
• Measuring cups
• Rubber spatula
• Resealable food-storage plastic bag (quart size)
• Scissors

**1** Heat the oven to 350°F.

**2** Count out 24 paper baking cups. Put 1 paper cup in each cup in the 2 muffin pans. Lightly spray the paper cups with the cooking spray.

**3** Measure out the water in the liquid measuring cup. Pour it into the custard cup. Measure out the oil in the liquid measuring cup. Crack 1 of the eggs on the edge of the bowl. Open the shell, letting the egg slide into the bowl. Do the same with the other eggs.

**4** To make and bake the cupcakes, follow the directions on the box using the water, oil and eggs. After baking the cupcakes, carefully take the muffin pans out of the oven with the pot holders and put them on the wire racks. Let the cupcakes cool for 20 minutes, until they aren't warm anymore.

**5** Take the wooden spoon and stick the handle down into the center of each of the cupcakes. Be careful not to go through the paper baking cup. Wiggle the wooden spoon around a little to make the hole about as wide as a penny. Take the wooden spoon out.

**6** Measure out the frosting. Scrape all of it out of the measuring cup with the rubber spatula and into the plastic bag. Seal the bag, leaving about 1 inch open. Use the scissors to cut a 1/2-inch hole in the bottom corner of the bag. Squeeze the bag to make the frosting come out of the hole in the bag and into the holes in the cupcakes. Poke 1 gummy worm partway into the frosting hole on top of each cupcake.

*1 Cupcake: Calories 200; Total Fat 8g; Sodium 160mg; Total Carbohydrates 30g (Sugars 24g); Protein 2g • Exchanges: 1 Starch, 1 Other Carbohydrate, 1 1/2 Fat*

**GOOD TO GO**
These cupcakes are a good dessert to pack in your lunch because the frosting is mostly inside the cupcake instead of on top.

# Create-a-Scene Cookie Puzzle

**TIME IT TAKES: 1 hour 50 minutes • HOW MUCH IT MAKES: 24 servings**

## INGREDIENTS

1 roll (18 ounces)
  refrigerated sugar
  cookie dough

3/4 cup vanilla ready-
  to-spread frosting

Desired gel or liquid
  food color

Small candies,
  chocolate chips,
  miniature
  marshmallows and/or
  raisins

## TOOLS YOU NEED

• Foil
• Pan (13 x 9 inch)
• Cutting board
• Sharp knife
• Pot holders
• Wire cooling rack
• Cookie cutters
• Large serving tray
• Measuring cups
• Small microwavable
  bowls
• Spoon
• Table knife

**1** Heat the oven to 350ºF.

**2** Tear off 1 piece of foil about 18 inches long and 12 inches wide. Turn the pan upside down. Cover the upside-down pan with foil. Press the foil down around the side of the pan. Take the foil off the pan. Turn the pan right side up. Now put the foil inside the pan, pushing it carefully into the bottom so the inside of the pan is completely covered with foil. Fold the top of the foil down over the edge of the pan.

**3** Remove the cookie dough from the wrapper. Put the dough on the cutting board. Use the sharp knife to cut it lengthwise and crosswise into 4 pieces. Put 1 chunk of dough in each of the 4 corners of the foil-lined pan. Press the dough down flat in the pan with your fingers. Smush the 4 pieces together until you have 1 giant rectangular cookie. (If your fingers get sticky, dip them in a little flour.)

**4** Bake the giant cookie for 15 to 20 minutes or until the edges look golden brown. Carefully take the pan out of the oven with the pot holders and put it on the wire rack. Cool the cookie in the pan for 20 minutes, until it isn't warm anymore. Put the pan in the freezer for 30 minutes.

**5** Take the pan out of the freezer. Carefully lift the giant cookie out of the pan by pulling up on the foil. Remove the foil from the cookie. Put the cookie on the tray.

**6** To make a puzzle, use the cookie cutter to cut a bunch of different shapes out of the giant cookie. Carefully remove the shapes from the giant cookie.

**7** Measure out the frosting. Decide how many different colors of frosting you want. Then divide the frosting with the spoon into that many small bowls. Add the gel or liquid food colors you want to the frostings. Stir the frostings until they are all mixed up. Microwave 1 bowl of frosting at a time for 5 to 10 seconds. Stir the frosting with the spoon until it is smooth.

**8** Use the table knife to spread the frosting on the cut-out shapes any way you want. Decorate the cut-out shapes with the candies, marshmallows, raisins and chips. Don't forget to spread the frosting on the background cookie, too. Let everything dry until the frosting is no longer wet. Then put the shapes back into the puzzle.

*1 Serving: Calories 130; Total Fat 4 1/2g; Sodium 70mg; Total Carbohydrates 22g (Sugars 16g); Protein 0g • Exchanges: 1/2 Starch, 1 Other Carbohydrate, 1 Fat*

# Fancy Dipped Strawberries

**TIME IT TAKES: 45 minutes • HOW MUCH IT MAKES: 40 strawberries**

## INGREDIENTS

### TOPPINGS
Miniature semisweet
chocolate chips
Chopped nuts
Colored sugars and
candy sprinkles
Grated chocolate
Shredded coconut

### DIPPED BERRIES
1 quart fresh whole
strawberries with
stems (4 cups)
1 cup vanilla ready-to-
spread frosting

## TOOLS YOU NEED
• Waxed paper
• Large cookie sheet
• Custard cups
• Colander
• Paper towels
• Measuring cups
• Rubber spatula
• Small deep
microwavable bowl
(1 1/2 cup)
• Spoon

**1** Tear off 1 piece of waxed paper. Put it on the large cookie sheet. Decide what toppings you want to put on your strawberries. Put some of each of the toppings you pick in a different custard cup.

**2** Put the colander in the sink. Put the strawberries in the colander. Rinse them with cold water. Put the washed strawberries on paper towels. Pat them dry.

**3** Measure out the frosting. Use the rubber spatula to scrape all of it out of the measuring cup and into the bowl. Microwave the frosting on High 15 to 20 seconds, until it is melted. Stir the frosting once with the spoon.

**4** Dip the bottom of the each strawberry halfway into the melted frosting. Right away, dip the strawberry into 1 of the toppings you picked. Put the strawberries on the waxed paper-lined cookie sheets. Put the cookie sheets in the refrigerator for 5 minutes or until the frosting on the strawberries is hard.

*1 Dipped Strawberry: Calories 50; Total Fat 2g; Sodium 0mg; Total Carbohydrates 8g (Sugars 8g); Protein 0g • Exchanges: 1/2 Fruit, 1/2 Fat*

**BLACK OR WHITE?**
Try dipping these scrumptious strawberries in chocolate frosting instead of the vanilla frosting.

# Glazed Brownie Hearts

**TIME IT TAKES:** 2 hours 20 minutes • **HOW MUCH IT MAKES:** 14 brownie hearts

## INGREDIENTS

### BROWNIES
1 box (19.8 ounces) fudge brownie mix
1/2 cup vegetable oil
1/4 cup water
2 eggs

### GLAZE
1 can (16 ounces) vanilla ready-to-spread frosting
Red food color
Multicolored candy sprinkles or colored sugar

## TOOLS YOU NEED
• Foil
• Pan (13 x 9 inch)
• Cooking spray
• Medium bowl
• Liquid measuring cup (1 cup)
• Wooden spoon
• Rubber spatula
• Pot holders
• Wire cooling rack
• Waxed paper
• Heart-shaped cookie cutter (2 1/2 inches in diameter)
• Small microwavable bowl (2 cup)
• Spoon

**1**  Heat the oven to 350ºF.

**2**  Tear off 1 piece of foil about 18 inches long and 12 inches wide. Turn the pan upside down. Cover the upside-down pan with foil. Press the foil down around the side of the pan. Take the foil off the pan. Turn the pan right side up. Now put the foil inside the pan, pushing it carefully into the bottom so the inside of each pan is completely covered with foil. Fold the top of the foil down over the edge of the pan. Spray the foil with cooking spray.

**3**  Pour the brownie mix into the medium bowl. Measure out the oil in the liquid measuring cup. Pour it into the bowl. Measure out the water in the same cup. Pour it into the bowl, too. Crack 1 of the eggs on the edge of the bowl. Open the shell, letting the egg slide into the bowl. (See the How-To Photo.) Do the same thing with the other egg. Stir everything in the bowl together with the wooden spoon, stirring around and around about 50 times until it's all mixed up.

**4**  Pour the batter from the bowl into the foil-lined pan. Scrape the inside of the bowl with the rubber spatula to get all the batter out of the bowl. Spread the top of the batter with the rubber spatula to make it smooth.

**5**  Bake the brownies for 28 to 30 minutes. Don't let them bake too long or they will get dry and tough. Carefully take the pan out of the oven with the pot holders. Put the pan on the wire rack. Let the brownies cool for 45 minutes.

**6**  When the brownies are cool, cover the pan of brownies tightly with another piece of foil. Freeze the brownies for 30 minutes so they get very cold.

**7**  Tear off 1 piece of waxed paper. The piece should be about 12 inches long and 12 inches wide. Put the waxed paper under the wire rack. Take the pan of brownies out of the freezer. Take off the foil on top of the pan. Carefully lift the cold brownies out of the pan by pulling up on the foil under the brownies. Flip the brownies upside down so the foil is now on top. Peel the foil off the brownies.

**8**  With the 2 1/2-inch heart-shaped cookie cutter, cut out 14 brownie hearts. Put the hearts on the wire rack over the waxed paper.

**LEFTOVERS TO LOVE**
Don't throw the brownie scraps out! Crumble them up and serve them over ice cream or pudding.

9  Use the rubber spatula to scrape all of the frosting out of the can and into the microwavable bowl. Microwave the frosting on High 30 to 40 seconds, until it is runny but not bubbling. Add a few drops of red food color. Stir with the spoon until it is all mixed up. If you want a darker pink frosting, stir in a few more drops of food color.

10  Carefully spoon the melted frosting over the tops of the brownie hearts. As soon as the brownie hearts are covered with frosting, sprinkle the candy sprinkles over the tops.

*1 Brownie Heart:* Calories 280; Total Fat 11g; Sodium 85mg; Total Carbohydrates 44g (Sugars 38g); Protein 1g • *Exchanges:* 1/2 Starch, 2 1/2 Other Carbohydrates, 2 Fat

# Double-Decker Malts

TIME IT TAKES: 50 minutes • HOW MUCH IT MAKES: 4 malts

## INGREDIENTS

1 pint vanilla ice cream
(2 cups)

1 pint chocolate ice
cream (2 cups)

1/2 cup malted milk
balls

1/2 cup milk

2 tablespoons malted
milk powder

Refrigerated whipped
cream topping from
an aerosol can

## TOOLS YOU NEED

• Measuring cups
• Resealable food-
  storage plastic bag
  (quart size)
• Rolling pin
• Blender with lid
• Liquid measuring
  cup (1 cup)
• 4 drinking glasses
  (8 ounces each)
• Measuring spoons

**1** Put both containers of ice cream in the refrigerator for 30 minutes to soften up the ice cream.

**2** Measure out the malted milk balls. Put them in the plastic bag. Smash the plastic bag with a rolling pin until the malted milk balls are broken into little pieces.

**3** If you need to, measure out the vanilla ice cream. Put it in the blender. Measure out 1/4 cup of the milk in the liquid measuring cup. Pour the milk into the blender, too. Put the lid on the blender. Blend until the mixture is smooth. Pour the mixture into the 4 glasses.

**4** Measure out 1 tablespoon smashed malted milk balls. Sprinkle them on top of 1 malt. Put the same amount of smashed malted milk balls on the other malts. Put the glasses in the freezer.

**5** Measure out the chocolate ice cream and 1/4 cup milk like you did in Step 2 with the vanilla ice cream and milk. Put them both in the blender. Measure out the malted milk powder. Add the powder to the blender, too. Put the lid on the blender. Blend until the mixture is smooth.

**6** Take the malts out of the freezer. Spoon the chocolate malt mixture evenly over the smashed malted milk balls in the glasses. Squirt about 2 tablespoons whipped cream topping on top of each malt. Sprinkle another 1 tablespoon of the smashed malted milk balls on each malt.

*1 Malt: Calories 380; Total Fat 19g; Sodium 160mg; Total Carbohydrates 47g (Sugars 37g); Protein 7g • Exchanges: 3 Starch, 3 Fat*

> **SCREAM FOR ICE CREAM**
> Feel free to use your favorite ice cream flavors instead of chocolate and vanilla. While you're at it, why not use your favorite candy topping, too?

# Frozen Brownie Sundae

**TIME IT TAKES:** 9 hours 50 minutes • **HOW MUCH IT MAKES:** 24 servings

## INGREDIENTS

### BROWNIE
1 box (19.8 ounces) fudge brownie mix
1/2 cup vegetable oil
1/4 cup water
2 eggs

### TOPPING
1 carton (1/2 gallon) chocolate chip-mint ice cream (8 cups), slightly softened
24 thin rectangular green and chocolate crème de menthe candies
1 jar (12 ounces) hot fudge ice cream topping

## TOOLS YOU NEED

• Pan (13 x 9 inch)
• Cooking spray
• Medium bowl
• Liquid measuring cup (1 cup)
• Wooden spoon
• 2 rubber spatulas
• Pot holders
• Wire cooling rack
• Ice cream scoop
• Sharp knife
• Pancake turner
• Dessert plates
• Measuring spoons

**1** Heat the oven to 350ºF.

**2** Spray only the inside bottom of the pan with cooking spray.

**3** Pour the brownie mix into the medium bowl. Measure out the oil in the liquid measuring cup. Pour it into the bowl. Measure out the water in the same cup. Pour it into the bowl, too. Crack 1 of the eggs on the edge of the bowl. Open the shell, letting the egg slide into the bowl. Do the same thing with the other egg. Stir everything in the bowl together with the wooden spoon, stirring around and around about 50 times until it's all mixed up.

**4** Pour the batter from the bowl into the pan. Scrape the inside of the bowl with a rubber spatula to get all the batter out of the bowl. Spread the top of the batter with the rubber spatula to make it smooth.

**5** Bake the brownies for 28 to 30 minutes. Don't bake them too long or they will get dry and tough. Carefully take the pan out of the oven with the pot holders. Put the pan on the wire rack. Let the brownies cool for 45 minutes.

**6** When the brownies are cool, scoop the softened ice cream out of the carton and put it on top of the brownies. Spread it over the brownies with the other rubber spatula until it is smooth. Put the pan in the freezer for at least 8 hours or overnight so the ice cream gets hard again.

**7** Take the dessert out of the freezer. Let it stand on the kitchen counter for 15 minutes. While the dessert get a little soft, unwrap the candies.

**8** Use the sharp knife to cut the dessert into squares. Use the pancake turner to remove the squares from the pan and put them on the plates. Measure out 1 tablespoon ice cream topping and pour it onto 1 dessert. Repeat putting topping on the other servings. Top each serving with 1 candy.

*1 Serving:* Calories 310; Total Fat 14g; Sodium 180mg; Total Carbohydrates 42g (Sugars 31g); Protein 4g • *Exchanges:* 1 Starch, 2 Other Carbohydrates, 2 1/2 Fat

**SPECIAL TREAT**
Make this extra-special dessert the next time you or someone in your family have something to celebrate. It looks super-fancy and tastes out of this world!

# Index

*Italicized pages references indicate photographs*